THE
SOCIOLOGY
OF
YOUTH

Simon Frith

Causeway Books

British Library Cataloguing in Publication Data

Frith, Simon
  The sociology of youth.—(Themes and
  perspectives in sociology)
  1. Children—Great Britain   2. Youth
  —Great Britain
  I. Title   II. Series
  305.2'3'0941   HQ792.G7

ISBN 0-946183-06-6

Published 1984
Reprinted 1986

Causeway Press Ltd.
PO Box 13, Ormskirk, Lancashire L39 5HP
© Causeway Press Ltd, 1984

Production by BPMS, Ormskirk.
Typesetting by Bookform, Formby, Merseyside
Printed and bound in England by Robert Hartnoll (1985) Ltd.,
Bodmin, Cornwall

Contents

Chapter Four
Youth as a Social Problem

Chapter Five
Sub-cultural Theory

Chapter Six
Critiques of Sub-cultural Theory

Chapter Seven
The Future of Youth

Bibliography

Index

Chapter One
Definitions

Is it necessary to devote a chapter to definitions of youth? Don't we all know who young people are? 'Youth' is not a term of sociological jargon. It is a common sense word, one we can find every day in the newspapers, hear every day in conversation. 'Youth', the dictionary says, 'is the state of being young'. What more do we need to know?

The sociological problems arise when we try to make such common sense thinking more precise. The dictionary provides a starting point – 'youth' describes an **age group**. People of a certain age are young and can be distinguished from people in other age groups – children, on the one hand, and adults, on the other. Theoretical sociologists don't often divide societies into age groups – they more often group people in terms of class and status, look at divisions of race and gender – but age categories are used in sociological research. Pick up books which use tables from social surveys, for example, and you will find people divided in terms of age: under 16, 16–24, 24–35, 35–45, and so on. So sociologists do draw on the common sense belief that people of different ages behave differently. There are problems though: aren't these age groupings arbitrary? Do 35 year-olds really have more in common with 25 year-olds than with 36 year-olds? Age differences are important but can they be treated so precisely?

This is the first question raised by the sociology of youth. Young people are people of a certain age, between childhood and adulthood, who form a significant social group, but it is difficult to define this age group precisely. At what age do children stop being children and become 'young people'? At what age do people become adult? It is tempting to lay down an arbitrary rule as in survey research: 'youth' means everybody between the ages of 11 and 20. But to proceed on the assumption that everyone in this age group behaves youthfully, is part of 'youth culture', brings us against valid common sense objections. Many 15 year-olds 'behave like children', many 18 year-olds behave like adults (are married and have children, for example).

'Youth', in other words, describes aspects of people's social position which are an effect of their biological age but not completely determined by it. If, for example, the end of youth is marked by our taking on an adult role – marriage and children, work and a career, our own household – then people stop being young at a great variety of ages.

The picture is even more complicated when we compare similar age groups in different societies or at different historical times. Everyone has to make the move from child to adult, but different societies at different times organise the move differently. The transition can take days or years, can mean being collected together with people of the same age or being kept apart from them; it can be a time of relative social freedom or repression. The task of the sociologist of youth is to show how particular societies organise the process of growing-up. For us, youth is not simply an age group, but **the social organisation of an age group**.

Dependence and Independence

One useful way of thinking about what it means to be young in Britain today is through this class exercise: write three headings on a piece of paper – child/youth/adult – and list underneath the social characteristics of each group. What becomes apparent immediately is that while it's easy enough to distinguish children and adults, it is less straightforward to differentiate young people from either. Young people **begin** not to be treated like children, **begin** to take on adult responsibilities, but this transition from child to adult doesn't happen evenly and is full of contradictions. The best way to think about young people is in terms of **dependency** and **responsibility**. I'll discuss dependency first. On the one hand, there are children, who are dependent, on the other hand, there are adults who have achieved independence. Youth describes the movement between the two – from dependence to independence. Young people have more independence than children (hence their common complaint to their parents: stop treating me like a child; I'm old enough now to choose my own clothes/go out by myself/come in late/have a boyfriend) but they are still dependent on adults for subsistence and knowledge, for love and security.

The concept of 'dependence' has to be related to particular insitutions:

a) **The Family**

'Youth' describes a family position and the central experience of growing up is that of becoming less dependent on our family (whatever form that family takes). The assumption in Britain is that children will eventually leave home, have families and households of their own. It follows that as the shape of the family changes so does the meaning of youth.

b) **Education**

The first obvious social move towards independence from their families comes when children go to school – whether play school, nursery or infant school. Schools are the only institutions which give people of the same age a common experience formally, which treat age with biological precision – we have to attend school from age 5 to 16 whatever the differences between us otherwise. But school life does change as pupils get older, it does involve their being given increasing individual responsibility for their school work and success or failure. Sixth-formers, attending school 'voluntarily' and organising their work around individually chosen A-Level subjects are more independent even at school than primary age children.

c) **Work**

Common sense suggests that school-leaving means the end of youth. When people enter the labour market, earn a wage of their own, aren't they taking on adult status? Young workers certainly have more independence than school pupils (or the young unemployed) but they are still involved in the move **towards** adult status. This is partly a matter of money – young people are paid less than adults; it is assumed that they still live with their parents, have no 'dependents' of their own. And it's partly a matter of the work-place itself. Young people going into skilled crafts need to be trained and as trainees or apprentices they remain under particular sorts of adult authority. Unskilled young workers too come under strict forms of discipline as they are 'socialised' into work habits. The young worker is regarded by employers as less reliable than the adult worker, more likely to misbehave, to change jobs out of boredom and restlessness – even at work there is a period of 'settling down'. Adult workers are not exactly 'independent' (and most young workers don't expect to become bosses) but young workers are, on the whole, more clearly subordinate.

d) **Leisure**

Youth culture, as we'll see, is particularly associated with leisure activities. It is how young people enjoy themselves (with clothes and music and dancing and hanging about) that makes them a distinct social group, and so most sociology of youth is, in fact, a sociology of youth leisure. This concentration on leisure can be misleading – how people enjoy their 'free time' can't be understood apart from their experience of family, education and work. Why, then, do sociologists of youth focus on leisure? Because it's in their free time that young people most **visibly** behave independently, express non-adult tastes and values. Leisure is, therefore, the most **accessible** site for research into youth behaviour – I'll discuss the methodological implications of this later.

Changing Responsibilities

The second important aspect of the transition from childhood to adulthood concerns the idea of 'responsibility'. Young people are often described as 'irresponsible' but youth is, in fact, the time when new responsibilities are continually being taken on – responsibilities for homework, for evening and weekend employment, for child-minding, examination study, leisure behaviour, and so on. This reflects young people's changing institutional roles, but it reminds us too that 'growing up' has psychological implications, involves intellectual and emotional developments. Young people are expected to 'mature', and if maturity is an even vaguer concept than youth, it lies, nevertheless, behind the most precise way in which society defines the youth/adult divide, with **the law**.

The law defines adulthood in terms of responsibility – people are legally adult when they are regarded by law as being responsible for their actions, when they are treated as mature enough to make certain sorts of decisions for themselves. The complication here is that different responsibilities are associated with different ages. As a class exercise, find out, for example, at what age people may legally:

- leave home
- leave school
- buy cigarettes
- buy alcoholic drinks
- drive a motor cycle
- drive a car
- marry
- consent to heterosexual activity
- consent to homosexual activity
- vote
- draw social security
- be charged in an adult court
- stand for parliament
- join the army
- go on a council house waiting list

Laws regulate all these activities and in doing so lay down precise legal distinctions between adult and youthful responsibilities. To be young, in other words, is partly a matter of legal definitions, and when the law changes (with the raising of the school leaving age from 15 to 16 or the lowering of the voting age from 21 to 18) so does the meaning of youth. But there's a final point to make: the law decides when we are **capable** of certain actions (and has to treat biological age as the best measure of this) but does not compel us to **accept** adult responsibilities. Most people marry, for example, several years after it is legally possible. This suggests a gap between legal and social definitions of adulthood and I'll return to the implications of this in chapter 4.

Youth and Social Differences

So far I've been discussing what young people have in common, but while they may therefore share problems of dependency in family, school and work, may be defined as equally responsible (or irresponsible) in legal terms, they face these problems from different institutional positions.

The most important difference among young people is the gender difference – growing up male and growing up female involve different activities, different constraints, different patterns of socialisation. This is not just a result of the sexual differences focused by puberty, but is a consequence too of boys' and girls' different roles in the family. As long as adult men and women are not equal (in terms of job opportunity and wages, for example) so women will be in some respects 'dependent' on men, and this obviously has consequences for girls' movement towards 'independence'. Similarly, men and women are seen to have different adult responsibilities which makes for different legal treatment of boys and girls, as I'll describe in chapter 4.

The second obvious difference among young people is in terms of social class which, in particular, affects people's experience of school and work. Sixteen year-old working class school leavers looking for jobs or places on Government training schemes are 'young' in different ways than sixteen year-old public school pupils getting ready to do A-Levels, to go to university, to get professional qualifications. The differences lie not just in day-to-day experiences but also in people's expectations about the future – young people cannot ignore the structure of power and wealth in our society and nor should we.

There are other significant social differences – racial differences, ethnic differences, even regional differences – consider the different effects on growing up of town and country life. They all raise the central question of the sociology of youth: what is the relative importance of the **similarities** between young people (in terms of dependency and irresponsibility) and the **differences** between them (in terms of gender, class and race). Is there one youth culture or are there many? I'll come back to this in chapter 2.

The Experience of Generation

The importance of the term 'generation' (as used by the sociologist Karl

Mannheim) is to draw attention to the fact that people grow up at particular historical moments and may, therefore, share crucial historical experiences with fellow members of their age group – experiences which then differentiate them, as a generation, from both older and younger generations. War is the most commonly cited experience that may bind a generation together, but rapid technological change and a boom/slump cycle in the economy may also have the effect of making an age group differentiate itself from older and younger people. Thus Britons who grew up in the depression years of the 1930s brought up children who took the boom years of the 1950s and 1960s for granted, but are now bringing up children to join the youth unemployment statistics of the 1980s. Such different experiences make for different assumptions and expectations about how society can and should work, and these differences may, in turn, be expressed in social conflicts, in a 'generation gap'.

Adolescence – Biology vs Sociology

If growing up is a psychological as well as a sociological process, it follows that youth, 'the state of being young', is a psychological as well as a sociological state. The concept of 'adolescence' was introduced by the American educational psychologist G. Stanley Hall at the beginning of this century to describe the emotional problems young people may face in managing the transition to adulthood, the break from their families, the development of independent personalities, and so on. Hall, like many other psychologists, believed that adolescence meant a period of particular 'storm and stress' emotionally, and while there is little sociological evidence to support this, it is worth noting the effects of the increasing **length** of adolescence. There is tension, for example, between the biological and sociological aspects of growing up – people are physically capable of sexual activity and enjoyment several years before this is socially acceptable, and one important function of youth culture is to manage the resulting problems, the issues of sexuality, attractiveness, friendship and love (think of the 'problems' that are addressed on the 'problem pages' of teenage girls' magazines).

The History of Youth: Industrialisation and the Separation of Home and Work

Why have the social and psychological conditions of youth become an issue in the last hundred years? The answer obviously lies in the increasing length of time of the transition from childhood to adulthood, but the question remains: why has the time of transition increased? The common sense answer to this is that as the division of labour has become more complex, the production process more technologically advanced, so adult roles need more preparation, more schooling. But in thus tracing the emergence of youth back to the Industrial Revolution, we find that the key to the need for a longer period of transition was not technology as such but **the separation of home and work** embodied in the factory system. This meant, first, that becoming adult involved leaving home, having an independent position in the labour market, and, second, that adult success rested on the possession of **formal** skills and qualifications. Peasants' children may expect to work on the family land, their occupation determined by their family position; factory workers' children have to find work for themselves. This was the setting in which childrens' education was taken out of their parents' hands, organised in schools. Historically as well as sociologically, then, youth, as an institution, is the product of the shifting relationships of family, school and work. With this in mind I want to turn now to the subject of this book: the sociology of **youth culture**.

Chapter Two
The Concept of Youth Culture

What is Culture?

'Culture' is a problematic word for sociologists and often seems to have as many meanings as there are people using it. Sociologists of youth tend to give it its most general sense, meaning 'a way of life'; youth culture is thus defined as 'the way of life shared by young people'. Having said this, though, it is important to add that such a definition of youth culture has been approached in two ways.

Youth culture can describe the particular pattern of beliefs, values, symbols and activities that a group of young people are **seen** to share. The starting point of this description is the empirical observation of young people's social life. Sociologists observe that certain youth groups – punks, for example – have distinct ways of dressing and doing their hair, listen to a particular form of music, develop their own slang and tastes, gather in particular places. The assumption is then made that shared activities reflect shared values, and the sociological task is to reveal these values, to get at the **meaning** of the observed behaviour. This has been, on the whole, the British approach to youth culture and I'll go into its methodological problems in my discussion of sub-cultural theory in chapter 5.

Youth culture can, alternatively, be approached in 'functionalist' terms. The starting point here is young people's shared institutional position, their consequent shared social problems. 'Youth culture' refers to the way these problems are solved in day-to-day practice, describes the values and activities that young people develop to make sense of and cope with their shared experiences – it has a 'problem-solving' function. This has, on the whole, been the American approach to youth culture and I'll examine its theoretical assumptions in more detail in the next chapter. Here I will outline how the empirical bases of both these approaches were established by sociologists in the 1950s.

Britain and the Discovery of the Teenage Consumer

The first influential sociological study of youth culture published in Britain was Mark Abrams's *The Teenage Consumer*, which appeared in 1959. Abrams was a market researcher and his book was an empirical survey of a new **consumer group**, which had emerged almost imperceptibly in the 1950s but was, by the end of the decade, vitally important for a wide range of companies making youth products. The importance of Abrams's book was that it described a distinctive form of youth behaviour that was not, in itself, delinquent – previously, 'youth culture', if used at all, carried intimations of street gangs and trouble. As a consumer group, young people were distinguished from other age groups not by their 'bad' behaviour, but simply in terms of their market choices, and it was these choices that revealed a new 'teenage culture'. This culture was defined in terms of leisure and leisure goods – coffee and milk bars, fashion clothes and hair styles, cosmetics, rock 'n' roll records, films and magazines, scooters and motorbikes, dancing and dance halls.

The definition of youth as a consumer group had two consequences. First, youth culture was interpreted as a form of **mass culture**. 'Mass culture' was a term developed by social commentators in the 1920s and 30s to describe the effects of the 'mass media' (large circulation newspapers and magazines, radio and gramophone records, cinema and advertising). It was a critical term, used by people hostile to the mass media for two reasons: first, because the media meant that people no longer made entertainment for themselves but relied on businessmen to provide it for them; second, because the media sought to appeal to the mass of the British people regardless of their particular local concerns and thus offered not accounts of people's real lives, but rather, empty fantasies that could appeal to everyone. Mass culture, in short, meant a form of culture in which people were **manipulated**, as consumers, by big business, and Abrams's research raised a question that is still often asked: is 'youth culture' really just the product of shrewd marketing men and advertisers?

Mass culture implies classless culture, a way of life (or consumption) that is shared by people in different social positions, but Abrams's research showed that the consumer habits of youth (which he defined as the period between school-leaving and age 25 or marriage) were dominated by its most affluent section, working class males. 1950s youth culture was thus interpreted as a form of **working class mass culture**. A distinction had to be made, in J. B. Mays' words 'between a culture largely based on working class peer group solidarity and the commercialised entertainment world, on the one hand, and the individualistic, middle class, school and university career system on the other'. 'Youth culture' referred initially, then, to 'working class peer group solidarity'.

Abrams's findings posed further problems for British sociologists. Why had teenage culture developed now, in the 1950s? The answer, it seemed, lay in the relative affluence of the decade. Young people were fully employed and had less obligation than previous generations to contribute their wages to the family income (their parents were in steady employment too). They had, in other words, a much greater 'disposable income' than people of their age had ever had before, and it was their disposable income that gave them their market power.

But a question remained: why did teenage spending take its particular form? Why did young people use their money differently from adults? Again, the answer seemed straightforward. The difference between adult and youthful consumers was that the young devoted their wages to 'short term hedonism', to leisure and pleasure. Their spending habits were a market expression of their lack of adult responsibiltiies and dependents.

The third issue was more complicated. Did young people's 'hedonism' mean that they had different values than their parents? Abrams's surveys showed that young people didn't just spend relatively **more** of their incomes on fashion clothes and pop records, but also that they spent their incomes on specifically **youthful** fashion clothes and pop records. Part of the pleasure of youth spending seemed to lie in its assertion of youth identity; it expressed the pleasure of **not being grown-up**! And this was why 'the teenage consumer' could be taken to be part of a 'teenage culture'.

What was the social importance of this culture? For some sociologists (including Abrams), youth spending revealed a distinct leisure group but didn't reflect any sort of 'rebellion'. Teenagers were still embedded in the key institutions of home, school and work; their central values remained those of their parents and workmates. As the National Children's Bureau's surveys have shown repeatedly since, 'the archetypal 16 year-old is a long way from the idle anarchistic teenager of legend. There is little evidence for the generation gap . . . Britain's future, in fact, appears to be in the hands of a remarkably conventional generation of young men and women not markedly different from the parents who worry about them'. (This was the *Observer*'s summary of the NCB's findings in 1976.)

For other sociologists, though, the development of a specific teenage market revealed the growing importance for young people of a **peer**

group world, unpenetrated by adult authority, dominated by group pressures and easily manipulated by commercial interests. This was the way that young street gangs had always been described, and the 1950s fear was that 'ordinary' youth might be drawn into such delinquent groups via teenage culture. Teddy Boys, the first spectacular post-war youth sub-culture were, then, a new sort of social problem. They were delinquents with a glamourous style – they offered **all** working class boys a desirable image. Observers concluded that teenage culture reflected not just relative affluence but also the decomposition of the pre-war working class community. From this perspective the social changes in post-war Britain – the rebuilding of slum neighbourhoods as housing estates, the increasing difference between the places where people lived and the places where they worked, the greater time young people spent at school – involved a weakening of the authority of working class parents over their children, of the old over the young.

Teenage culture thus filled the gap left by the decreasing relevance of traditional norms of youth behaviour. Parents couldn't give their children convincing advice on how to behave as teenagers because they'd never been teenagers, in this affluent, consumer sense, themselves. And so, as I've already suggested, Mark Abrams's market research measured a mass teenage culture, a pattern of tastes and expenditure which went beyond neighbourhood and community ties and traditions. Working class teenagers in Sunderland, it seemed, wore the same styles, listened to the same records, had the same day-dreams as working class teenagers in London or Scotland or South Wales. 'Teenage' culture was, indeed, a form of American culture. Even Teddy Boys combined their Edwardian look with fashions taken from Hollywood – the city slicker's string-tie, the Western gambler's side-burns and frock coat. And they (like all other British working class teenagers) listened to American music, to rock 'n' roll. The very idea of the 'teenager' was, for many British adults, an alien, American idea, involved American myths, American idols, fantasies of American life.

The USA and the Discovery of an Adolescent Society

The image of American youth culture that British teenagers got from rock 'n' roll records and films was first formed, in fact, in the 1920s. It was then, for example, that motor-cars began to be used by wealthy youngsters as a way of escaping family supervision, that courting became 'dating', no longer directly chaperoned by adults, that the use of make-up and cigarettes ceased to be the mark of the 'bad girl', that the mass media (Hollywood films, in particular) began to shape young people's sense of their social possibilities.

What lay behind these first intimations of a youth culture was the accelerated separation of home and work. Middle class parents' influence over their children's decisions about careers and education, sex and marriage, leisure and consumption, declined. The high school and college began to replace the family as the centre of middle class youth's social life, the source of their moral values. By the late 1930s American sociologists like the Lynds were observing in small town high schools 'a self consicous sub-culture of the young'.

At this time a clear distinction could still be drawn between middle class school culture and working class street culture, but in the 1950s the high school became the social centre of the lives of most young Americans and the resulting concept of the 'teenager' blurred class distinctions. In Britain in the 1950s, as we've seen, 'youth culture' meant working class youth culture, but in the USA the term covered **both** 'rough' street group activities **and** 'respectable' school group activities (so that, for example, in the television series *Happy Days*, which looks back to 1950s youth culture, The Fonz is a street figure **within** the school). The adult worry was that teenage culture would dissolve not just class distinctions but also the differences between 'conformist' and 'delinquent' youth of both classes, and American sociologists concentrated research on this problem. 'Youth culture' was seen to be the setting for both deviant and conformist teenagers, for both 'corner' and 'college' boys (I will discuss this further in chapter 4) and it became too the setting for attempts to **control** the young.

Adults – teachers, parents, religious leaders, social workers, the police – sought to counter juvenile delinquency not by competing with youth culture but by institutionalising it, using the rules of conduct first developed by middle class teenagers in schools and colleges in the 1920s and 1930s. One result of these attempts to **intervene** in youth culture was that American sociologists developed a much more complex understanding than British sociologists of 'the adolescent society' (the title of James Coleman's definitive study which came out in 1961). Their focus was not consumer choice but the ways in which adolescent behaviour was a response to specific problems posed at home and school and work. Youth culture was understood not as an expression of **autonomous** teenage values, but as something which could be used by adults to promote the **right** attitudes.

In both sociological and popular literature on 1950s American teenagers a confused picture began to emerge. On the one hand there was the **teenager-as-rebel** – captured in films like *Rebel Without A Cause, The Wild Ones* and *The Blackboard Jungle*, in rock 'n' roll stars like Elvis Presley, Gene Vincent and Jerry Lee Lewis, in the ubiquitous image of the slouched, leather-clad, mumbling street corner gang. On the other hand there was the **teenager-as-all-American**, drinking Coca-Cola on the beach, dancing at the high school hop, playing football and cheer-leading, clean-cut and cheerful. If the delinquent image had the exaggerated lines of a 'moral panic' (see chapter 4), the high school image was equally a stereotype, an attempt to make teenagers **nice**, to control their culture by encouraging the right sort of competition (football games not gang fights), fun (cruising to the drive-in rather than getting drunk or drugged) and sex (which was regulated by elaborate codes of 'dating' and 'petting'). This teenage ideal didn't spring to life spontaneously but was deliberately fostered in a plethora of magazines, songs and television programmes which clearly placed teenagers' short-term pleasures in the long-term framework of middle class family life.

What is most striking about such 1950s teenage ideology is its concern with rules. The joy of teenage life was said to be its 'freedom' (and that television series is, after all, called *Happy Days*). A typical 1950s book for girls, Connie Francis's *For Every Young Heart*, thus begins, 'Have a ball – no strings attached! That's privilege number one in the Teenage Bill of Rights!' But the rest of the book consists of rules of dress and make-up, family and sexual behaviour (rules which can still be found laid out in the pages of British girls' magazines, like *Jackie*). What American writers realised was that youth culture wasn't **static** (a set of values to be read off teenage goods) but **dynamic** – young people had to **learn** to be 'teenagers' (and adults could therefore help teach them). As the British sociologist Tom Kitwood has argued more recently, 'becoming a teenager' can be an anxious and unhappy process. If there are rules of teenage behaviour then they can be inadvertently broken. Young people grow up by making mistakes; they can feel themselves oppressed by their peers as well as supported by them. I'll return to the implications of this in chapter 6.

Adults and Teenagers: Anxieties and Envy

Sociologists in both Britain and the USA in the 1950s found that adults had an extremely ambiguous attitude towards teenage culture. They were remarkably tolerant of their own children, asserting that youth was a time 'for sowing wild oats', that 'boys will be boys', telling their daughters 'to have a good time while you can'. But they were decidedly intolerant of other people's children, dismissing the young as 'undisciplined, oversexed layabouts'.

This confusion of attitudes has a long history. Even in the nineteenth century youth was both **celebrated** – as a time of innocence and idealism, when all life's choices can still be made – and **condemned** – as a time of anarchy and hysteria, irresponsibility and selfishness. The 1950s rise of a commercial teenage culture focused these contradictions. As teenagers developed their own distinct **public** institutions and means of expression, they became more feared and more envied. By the end of the decade, indeed, young people had become, in themselves, **symbols** of certain sorts of general pleasure (and risk). To be young was to be associated with consumption, fashion, pop and fun. The implication was that adults could be young this way too – by equally committing themselves to consumption, fashion, pop and fun. 'Youth' became a sales ideal for grown-ups. In advertisements and films and music young people were used to stand for 'freedom' to represent 'good times'. By the mid-1960s, as American sociologists like Bennett Berger began to observe, 'youth culture' had become as much a product of adult as of teenage concerns. It was an **ideological** concept, defining an **ideal** 'way of life'.

The Rise of 'Youth Culture'

In 1950s Britain the terms 'youth culture' and 'teenage culture' were pretty much interchangeable – both referred to working class youngsters. Middle class youth were thought to make sense of their lives by reference to a longer-term idea of career and achievement. But as youth culture became increasingly an ideological matter, referring to leisure ideals as well as realities, so it became attractive for middle class teenagers too, and it was the gradual appropriation of the trappings of working class teenage consumer culture by the middle classes which quickly came to be thought of as British 'youth culture' (often, understandably if misleadingly, described in terms of **classlessness**).

This was most obvious in the development of pop music – a development neatly symbolised by the sleeve covers of the Beatles' first two LPs: on the first they are obviously working class, chirpy in their best suits, on the second they have become solemnly middle class, dressed in student sweaters. By the end of the 1960s British record companies divided their market into 'pop' and 'rock' – pop records still played their traditional role in working class teenage leisure, but they were outsold now by rock LPs, and 'youth culture' no longer meant the pop scene but, rather, the rock world of 'progressive' musicians, student audiences, 'serious' fans. Abrams's affluent school leavers no longer dominated the youth market. Youth culture increasingly meant student culture – by 1967 the Beatles, still the British youth model, were hippies, part of the psychedelic underground.

Middle class youth culture was, from the start, more **self-consciously** 'rebellious' than working class youth culture. Even in the 1950s American sociologists had suggested that in becoming rock 'n' roll fans middle class children were often deliberately adopting what they perceived as lower-class values – 'toughness, excitement, chance-taking, indulgence' – and were, thereby, consciously **opposing** their parents. Working class children, by contrast it seemed, were simply enjoying themselves before settling down conventionally. They might **drift** into delinquency but such 'rebellion' was a matter of confusion, the **lack** of adult discipline. The solution to this youth problem was to regulate peer group culture, to provide the missing norms. 1960s youth culture, by contrast, increasingly articulated the **rejection** of such norms.

Student Movements and Counter-Cultures

The argument that middle class youth were intrinsically more 'political' than even 'deviant' working class youth was challenged by sub-cultural theorists in the 1970s (see chapter 5) but in the late 1960s it seemed common sense. For middle class teenagers – sixth formers and college students, trainee professionals and managers – to indulge in 'short term hedonism' was to challenge their parents' commitment to career planning and 'deferred gratification' (working hard in the present for rewards in the future). For middle class children to engage with 'pop culture' was to threaten their parents' carefully guarded status and 'respectability'. Not surprisingly, young people in both Britain and the USA experienced youth culture as a form of 'liberation' – liberation from the stuffy expectations of their teachers and families (and the resulting 'generation gap' was reinforced by the availability of the contraceptive pill, which gave young women a new sort of sexual freedom). Youth, in short, were the vanguard of the 'permissive' society.

Middle class youth culture didn't develop in an institutional vacuum. 1950s youth culture was rooted in young workers' leisure behaviour; 1960s youth culture was set in the schools and colleges which 'successful' children could expect to attend into their twenties. This had two political consequences.

First, students are in more formally organised age groups than other young people; they have more formal means of expression – student unions, student newspapers, student representatives. Colleges provide too an immediate **target** for student politics. 1960s youth culture involved, then, student campaigns against school rules, against college discipline and control of leisure activities. But attention soon shifted to more important matters, to the organisation of knowledge and educational power itself, as students demanded some influence over their curriculum, over examinations. What emerged from such demands was an explicit **student movement**. This took different forms in different places, but all Western countries (and some Eastern ones) had 1960s experience of student sit-ins, demonstrations, campaigns and protest.

Middle class young people became, in a sense, the political conscience of their countries, protesting against adult activities in which they were not yet implicated (even if their parents were) – thus it was **young** people who marched with Civil Rights demonstrators in the US South, **young** Britons who demonstrated their support of CND or the anti-Vietnam War movement.

The second political consequence flowed from this. Middle class youth culture involved older, more articulate people than working class youth culture, expressed a specific **refusal** to settle down, to behave like adults. This refusal increasingly took the form of a **counter-culture**, as young people not only rejected adult institutions but practiced **alternative** ways of growing up – play not work, drugs not drink, communes not marriage. The hippies became the symbols of the counter-culture, and in hippies' 'underground' activities we can see the seeds of 1970s 'alternative' politics – women's, gays' and animals' liberation, squatting and do-it-yourself entertainment, ecology and Greenpeace. But the immediate impact of hippie culture (which was, in important respects, developed as much on the streets as on the campuses) was on working class youth. By the end of the 1960s, 'youth culture' seemed to have moved full circle: working class youth behaviour had 'radicalised' middle class youth attitudes and now middle class youth behaviour was radicalising working class youth attitudes. In Paris in May 1968 it was the **combination** of students' and young workers' protests that faced the French government with a political crisis.

The Politics of Age: Is Youth an Interest Group?

1968 events, not just in France but around the world, raised pressing sociological questions. Was there now a youth **interest** group? Was there now a set of activities and values which, on the one hand, distinguished young people from adults and, on the other hand, gave them an identity that transcended their own class differences? Had youth culture become a **political** force?

The positive answer to these questions – the answer yes – rested on a historical argument. Young people, it was suggested, had been drawn together politically by economic affluence, by an expansion of higher education which involved more and more of them in technical training and bureaucratic routine. All young people, it was suggested, faced adult constraints over their use of drugs and noise and public places; all young people resented the attempts to turn them into well-regulated producers and orderly consumers.

Such arguments didn't long survive the 1970s recession and rise of youth unemployment. Systematic rather than impressionistic sociological surveys quickly confirmed that there were important cultural differences between young members of different social classes whatever their shared interest in personal freedom. In retrospect it seems clear that the brief 1960s moment of cross-class youth solidarity has to be related to more specific historical factors than 'affluence'. In the USA, certainly, the Vietnam War was something that affected all young people one way or another via the draft (and the efforts to avoid it). More nebulously, 1960s young people had expectations (and this was an effect of the relative economic prosperity) which gave them a shared interest in change for its own sake, a shared excitement at the feeling (whether in France or Czechoslovakia) that power structures could be broken. When they weren't, the excitement faded.

One sociological conclusion can be drawn from this, though. Arguments about the politics of youth must be given a proper context. The question 'is youth an interest group?' raises different issues in the 1980s than it did in the 1960s. Now we'd have to look at cross-class experiences of unemployment (not full employment), at new forms of education and training. I will do this in chapter 7. Next I want to outline an alternative approach to youth as an institution, an approach which considers these issues in terms not of social history but of social **function**.

Chapter Three

Functionalist Explanations of Youth Culture

What is Functionalism?

The functionalist approach to sociology begins with the idea that a society, a social structure, is like a body, a biological structure. Social institutions can then be explained in the same way that biologists explain parts of the body: by reference to their **function** in keeping the society (the body) alive. Biologists assume that every part of the body – the liver and the kidney, hair and toe-nails – has, or has had, a vital function. Organs may lose their function (and eventually wither away) as biological structures evolve, but nothing exists for no biological reason at all. Functionalist sociologists assume, similarly, that every social institution has, or has had, a social function, that history is best understood in terms of social evolution. Social structures change by becoming more complex, social institutions change by becoming more 'specialised'.

The most controversial of the functionalists' arguments is that social institutions must be explained in terms of their contribution to social stability. Biologists explain parts of the body in terms of the maintenance of life and so, following the biological analogy, functionalists relate social institutions to the maintenance of society. The implication is that an institution that was not functional in these terms, that disrupted social life and was **dysfunctional** would not survive for long. The converse also applies: an established social institution that appears disruptive must, in fact, help to maintain the social order (thus Durkheim argued that crime, as a 'normal' social phenomenon, must have a social function).

In the 1950s functionalists studied American teenage culture with these arguments in mind. They began with the assumption that youth culture (however delinquent some of its forms) had a social function, had appeared because changes in the American social structure had posed new problems that youth culture solved. The sociological task was to describe **what** function youth culture played in the maintenance of social order and to show **how** it performed that function. But there was also a further question implied: for **whom** was this function performed?

Functionalist sociology usually describes institutions as functioning for 'society' but we can also look at the way in which institutions function **for their members** – marriage, for example, contributes to the maintenance of social order, but also has a function for the people who get married (which is why they do so). The same point can be made about youth culture. The functionalist approach means explaining its function not just for society as a whole but also for the young people who live the culture for themselves.

Youth and the Social Structure: On the Margins

The functionalist approach to youth was first sketched out by the American sociologist Talcott Parsons during the Second World War, in a discussion of the role of age groups in society. However it was given its most systematic treatment in S. N. Eisenstadt's 1956 book, *From Generation To Generation* and it is his argument that I'll summarise here.

Eisenstadt begins by pointing out that in all societies children have to be 'socialised' before they can attain full adult status. They have to be taught their society's moral code, its common sense, its rules of behaviour; they have to be given the skills and knowledge necessary to perform their adult roles (and so socialisation may vary according to children's gender and class). In 'primitive' societies the values that inform the lives of children within their families are much the same as those that will organise their adult lives and so the change of status from child to adult is not particularly problematic. Even adult skills and knowledge are acquired 'naturally', as part of the experience of growing up, and so the moment of transition to adulthood is just a matter of ritual – a puberty or initiation rite. 'Youth' doesn't really exist.

In modern industrial societies, by contrast, there is a significant structural gap between the family in which children are brought up and the economic and social system in which they must eventually take their place. The shift of status from child to adult is neither quick nor easy, it means a lengthy period of transition and youth becomes an important structural position. Society has become more complex (the necessary consequence of social evolution) and new specialised institutions are needed to maintain it. As the family unit becomes concentrated on emotional and sexual (rather than economic) functions, so new institutions are necessary to handle other aspects of socialisation, to manage the move **out** of the family. Youth culture, in short, has to be understood by reference to the process in which a modern industrial society detaches children from their families and places them in/prepares them for the wider social system.

Eisenstadt emphasises two aspects of this process. First, the young have a **marginal** social status. Young people at school or college, in apprenticeships and as trainees, in and out of unskilled work, are not yet fully integrated into the economic structure; they have emerged from one family but not yet formed another, they are not yet fully integrated into the social structure. Their legal status (as we saw in chapter 1) is confused; even their 'free time' is regulated by adult authorities.

Second, industrial societies have developed a series of formal training institutions to control the transition period: not just schools, apprenticeships, colleges, and other overt forms of education, but also organisations, like youth clubs, and media products, like youth magazines, to train people in the norms and expectations of adult 'private' life, to prepare people for marriage and parenthood, for being householders and citizens. Whatever the differences between them in other respects, all young people have to be socialised, find themselves in socialising institutions and they share, consequently, a sense of subordination. These institutions may be **for** the young but they are not controlled **by** them. They are run by adults; young people are central to their purpose but marginal in terms of power.

The Function of Youth Culture: Managing Transitions

Shared experiences make for shared needs. Eisenstadt argued that young people seek a sense of stability to offset the experience of change, a sense of self-esteem to offset the experience of powerlessness. Youth culture is the result. It provides a clear set of values, attitudes and behavioural norms to follow whatever else is going on; by acting on youth cultural rules young people can feel good whatever anyone else thinks of them. Punks, for example, may look funny to passers-by or *News of the World* photographers, but to become a punk is to achieve a measure of success and status which is **under one's own control**.

Functionalists explain social institutions in terms of social problems and cultural solutions. The problem is described with reference to strains within the social structure; the solution is described in terms of the easing of such strains. The youth 'problem' lies, then, in young people's marginal status; youth culture eases the resulting anxieties and uncertainties. The sociological importance of youth culture lies in their **codes** of conduct and dress. The significance of punk, for example, is less its content – **what** people wear and do – than its form – the fact that there is a punk uniform, a punk version of success and prestige. From this perspective, **all** forms of youth culture (student rugby clubs as well as skinhead football gangs) have the same function.

The 'problem solving' approach to youth culture is used by many sociologists who would not consider themselves functionalists. Sub-culturalists, for example, also explain youth culture in terms of its solution to young people's problems (see chapter 5). They place a different emphasis, though on the question of for **whom** the culture is functional. For sub-culturalists, some young people are clearly **more** powerless than others, **more** marginal to the social order. Children who are school failures are more committed to alternative sources of status than school successes; youngsters in boring jobs are more committed to the leisure pursuit of risk and excitment; teenagers who don't expect to have much economic or cultural power when they become adults are more committed to the control now of whatever space they've got. The youth 'problem', in other words, can't be divorced from adult problems; youth cultures don't all have the same relationship to the social structure.

I'll come back to this point, but first it's worth stressing that Eisenstadt's position reflects his starting question: how does youth culture work to maintain social order? His argument is that in meeting young people's needs (which may well vary across classes) youth culture has the **general** function of smoothing the transition from child to adult. The important point for Eisenstadt is not that some young people become 'deviants' (punks, for instance), but that most 'deviant' youths become 'normal' adults. On the whole youth marginality has **not** been the cause of either political rebellion or lasting psychological problems. Despite moments of riot and counter-culture, contemporary industrial societies do succeed in socialising each new generation, in keeping society going as its members change.

Eisenstadt argued that youth culture's most important function for its members was emotional – it mattered in psychological rather than economic or political terms (he was writing before the rise of the student movement). This was the clue to its social function. The primary importance of 1950s youth culture, he suggested, was not to provide teenagers with a set of **norms** (which may or may not accord with adult values) but was, rather, to give them a set of **relationships**. Youth culture was a way of managing the psychological tensions involved in adolescence, a way of coping with the emotional shifts made necessary by the movement out of the intimate world of the family into the public world of school and work. The most significant aspect of youth culture, then, was its basis in the activities of **peer groups**.

The Importance of Peer Groups

Peer groups are so taken for granted by sociologists that it is sometimes easy to forget that references to youth culture are usually references to people of the same age doing things in groups – whether those groups are described as gangs or cliques or sub-cultures. Youth cultural activity means group activity. The sociological assumption is that young people develop their tastes in clothes and music **in groups**, that they watch football matches and go dancing, hang around the bus stop and 'do nothing' **in groups**. In the 'adolescent society', argued Coleman, people belong to very clearly defined social networks; they organise their behaviour round these networks' rigid systems of value and prestige.

Eisenstadt, though, was less interested in the content of peer groups – what particular norms they adopted – than in their **form**, in the **sort** of social interaction they involved. A peer group, he suggested, is charac-terised by friendship and loyalty, by people's commitment to each other because of **who** they are rather than because of **what** they represent. In social psychological terms, the peer group lies somewhere between the family (with its ties of absolute emotional commitment) and the economic system (with its formal contracts, its organisation of roles by reference to achieved skills and qualifications). To use Eisenstadt's language, the peer group manages the move from 'particularistic' to 'universalistic' values, from a social world in which decisions are made by reference to parental authority and family tradition to a social world in which decisions must be referred to universally agreed rational principles.

Peer groups, in short, support young people's initial steps out of family life, give them their first introduction to other ways of treating the social world. At the beginning this may simply be a matter of comparison (which leads children to argue with their parents – 'But *Karen's* mother lets her go to discos...') but as peer group activities become the centre of young people's social life, so they become the chief reference point for young people's behaviour. Peer groups enable their members to assert their independence of their families while still being able to depend on friendship and emotional support whatever they do. The functionalists' point is that peer groups matter as a source not of new **values** but of a new way of **placing oneself in the world**. They cease to matter once adult status is achieved. People 'grow out' of youth culture as they establish a new, exclusive form of emotional tie (marriage, their own families) and as they become identified with an occupational or career position. The social and psychological problems of growing up cannot be separated from each other. Youth culture itself only becomes a problem when people refuse to grow up and this (as sociologists like Talcott Parsons argued in the 1960s) needs a psychological rather than a political explanation.

Critiques of Functionalism: Are All Young People The Same?

Eisenstadt's argument is a general argument. It refers to the problem of transition that faces **all** young people in industrial society. The most telling criticism of his approach addresses this assumption. Are young people really all the same? Can 'youth culture' be used to describe a single institution, one that includes **everyone** in the relevant age group?

In an important article published in 1968 ('Some theoretical problems in the study of youth'), Sheila Allen argued that in capitalist societies, at least, the experiences of different **classes** occupying different economic situations, with different amounts of power, different sorts of access to educational reward, cannot be the same **at any age**. Sociologists would, these days, extend the argument. In patriarchal societies, at least, the experiences of different **genders** occupying different economic situations, with different amounts of power, different sorts of access to educational reward, cannot be the same at any age either. Growing up middle class is still a different process than growing up working class, and growing up male is a different process than growing up female. The sociology of youth culture must be able to make sense of these differences. Functionalists, Allen suggests, cannot.

The point is that if we examine youth cultures carefully we find not only sharply contrasting consumer tastes and choices, but also, more importantly, contrasting **constraints** on people's cultural activities. These constraints reflect people's class and gender positions as well as their age. Leisure activities, in short, are not really 'free' – they relate to people's position in the family and in the labour market. Leisure patterns, to put it another way, reflect leisure opportunities, and different groups of young people have different opportunities. Boys and girls use their 'free' time differently partly because they are 'free' in different ways. Girls have greater domestic obligations than boys, for example, and they seem to have a greater interest in using leisure as a means to marriage, as a way of 'finding the right boy'. I'll return to the implications of this in chapter 6.

Sociologists have, in general, shown that there are patterned differences in youth behaviour between students and young workers, between the skilled and the unskilled, the employed and the unemployed, between blacks and whites and Asians. To treat all these groups as part of the **same** youth culture is to argue at a high level of abstraction – what these young people all share are the 'psycho-social' problems of making the transition from childhood to adulthood in an industrial society, as Eisenstadt argued. But the **differences** in how such problems are experienced and resolved (or not resolved) are just as important, and it is such differences I'll be considering in the rest of this book. One particular contrast needs a note here, though.

Growing up British vs Growing up American

In recent years Kings Road, Chelsea, has become a favourite spot for American tourists. They go there to take pictures of Britain's 'youth tribes' (*Time* magazine's description) – punks, skinheads, teds, rockers, mods, rockabillies, new romantics. These tribes have members in the USA (and the rest of Europe), but they are a peculiarly British phenomenon and point to an interesting paradox: in the 1950s the USA was clearly the model for teenage fashion, teenage music and teenage culture, now Britain seems to set the styles. How can we explain youth cultural history in these two 'modern industrial societies'? Why have the British produced such a dramatic series of spectacular youth sub-cultures?

There are two obvious reasons. First, a much higher proportion of American youth continues in full time education after the age of 16. Their activities have a formal, student setting. British school leavers, by contrast, have to create their own youth spaces and identities. Second, social mobility is greater (or is thought to be greater) in the USA. American teenagers seem to believe in the possibility of changing their lives (if only by moving across the country) for much longer than British teenagers, who thus, again, have a greater need to dramatise their duller local identity. It is noticeable that the American youth groups which do put a premium on style and fashion, the blacks and the hispanics, are the American youth groups with the most restricted educational and occupational opportunities.

I'm mentioning this here in order to make my final point about the functionalist approach to youth culture. Like all sociological theories it must be related to its historical circumstances – in this case the 1950s. It was explaining youth culture in a time of relative affluence and optimism. If youth culture was, therefore, 'functional' this was, in part, because growing up wasn't a particularly problematic thing to do – people looked forward to the future. In other circumstances youth cultures carry different meanings, raise different problems. It is to these which I will now turn.

Chapter Four
Youth as a Social Problem

Hooliganism – The History of a Moral Panic

In his important book, *Hooligan*, Geoffrey Pearson tells the story of juvenile delinquency backwards, focusing on **reactions** to young criminals. He begins in the present, quoting contemporary newspapers' and politicians' arguments that delinquency is getting out of hand, that tough forms of discipline and punishment are urgently needed. These editors and MPs remember the law abiding 1950s, a time before youth culture, the permissive society and comprehensive education had undermined traditional family and school discipline. The problem, it seems, is that in the last twenty years the young have lost their 'respect for authority'.

Curious about this, Pearson turns to newspapers' and politicians' 1950s discussions of delinquency and finds exactly the same arguments! Then, too, it was believed that there was a hooligan crisis, that the young lacked discipline, that war and the welfare state had undermined the moral certainties of the 1930s. In search of a time when delinquency wasn't a problem, Pearson moves back to 1930s discussions and finds the same fears much in evidence, 'good behaviour' now being referred to the turn of the century, while at the turn of the century people referred back to the 1850s as the golden age of law and order, agitated about the new 'hooligan' problem.

Pearson takes his history back even further, but this summary does enough to establish two important sociological points. First, youth has been seen as a 'social problem' for at least a hundred years, certainly since groups of working class boys were first observed hanging around the streets, getting into 'trouble' with the police and other passers-by. Second, in describing youth as a problem, we are describing not just youth behaviour but also adult responses to it. We have to be able to make sense of 'respectable fears' (Pearson) and 'moral panics' (Stanley Cohen).

Delinquency, Disorder and Contamination

If we look back at the nineteenth century response to juvenile delinquency, examine the offences for which young people could be sentenced to periods in reform schools, it is clear that while the young were often criminal in adult ways (were robbers, for example) there were also offences that were exclusively youthful, that called forth a distinctive legal response.

The young, for example, were seen to be the source of a particular sort of **disorder**. Gangs of boys on the streets engaged in destructive and violent behaviour ('hooliganism' and 'vandalism') that had no apparent material ends, that didn't provide the boys with goods or cash. Hooliganism seemed to be enjoyed for its own sake, and hooligan gangs were a source of **contamination** – innocent youngsters were being drawn into their activities, cut off from adult influence and criminalised. Put these two problems together and it seemed obvious to nineteenth century politicians that the state had the right to control youth behaviour, to break up gangs, put 'idle' youths into custody **even if they hadn't actually broken the law**. The streets were a breeding ground for crime and criminals and the state therefore had the right to remove young people from them, to **reform** gang members.

From the beginning, then, 'juvenile delinquency' described a law and order problem that was different from the law and order problem posed by adult criminals. Three issues were involved in particular.

First, is delinquency a **collective** or an **individual** problem? The law defines crime in individual terms – this is the logic of arrest, trial and sentence – but much juvenile delinquency takes place in groups. Football hooliganism, for example, is a problem because of the activities of **groups** of people, but the law can only deal with those individuals 'unlucky' enough to be picked out of the crowd by the police.

Second, is delinquency a **rational** or **irrational** activity? Vandalism, for, example, is usually described by newspapers as 'mindless', football hooligans are called 'animals'. How can a 'rational' legal system respond to irrational behaviour?

Third, should the treatment of delinquents emphasise **punishment** or **reform**? Do young people need a clear **deterrent** from delinquency, 'a short sharp shock'? Or is the problem one of poor socialisation so that what is necessary is re-education?

These issues have particularly concerned sociologists and if, as a result, the sociology of youth has been dominated by studies of problem youth, then this is because such studies are seen to have **practical** implications. If sociologists can explain juvenile delinquency then they can have a direct influence on the state's youth policy.

Explaining Juvenile Delinquency – The 'Psycho-Dynamic' Approach

Juvenile crime was first seen as a problem when criminology was dominated by **positivism**. Positivist criminologists like Cesare Lombroso believed that 'criminality' was an inherent quality of criminals who were different sorts of people than non-criminals. He suggested that the inherent, genetic, **disposition** towards crime must have physical signs too, which could be discovered by **measuring** every aspect of convicted criminals and seeing what they had in common. It would then be possible to reduce the crime rate by recognising people with criminal tendencies even before they did anything wrong.

There are two difficulties in applying this approach to juvenile crime. First, delinquency involved group behaviour – could criminal groups be treated as 'diseased' in the same way as criminal individuals? Second, there was a political reluctance to treat children and young people as **doomed** to crime by their genes. Couldn't they be re-socialised and reformed? The positivist criminologists soon combined their biologistic approach with a concern for the role of the **social environment** in causing (and curing) criminality.

The most influential of these theorists in Britain was **Cyril Burt**, whose mammoth study, *The Young Delinquent*, was published in 1925. His starting point was that delinquency was a form of **moral subnormality**, but he concluded from his survey of delinquents in London that such subnormality had 'a multiplicity of contributory factors', varying from criminal parents to spending too much time in the cinema. Burt sought to organise these factors in order of importance and the result was a **psycho-dynamic** explanation. If delinquency reflected people's inability to follow rules and act responsibly, then this inability had to be referred to people's emotional and moral development. Genetic factors were certainly relevant to this, but the key to healthy moral growth was the **family** – Burt's study provided the evidence for the common sense view that juvenile delinquency is caused by 'bad families' and 'broken homes'.

Burt's approach was immediately influential and it continues to be applied in general terms by both criminologists and educational psychologists. What has changed is the definition of 'delinquency' involved. D. J. West's *The Young Offenders* (1967), for example, concludes that 'most convicted youth are ordinary youth', and that 'since so many delinquents are quite ordinary youngsters, it is reasonable to suppose that their behaviour represents the normal response of their age group to everyday circumstances'. Most delinquents, in short, are **not** morally subnormal. But West does then refer to 'the hard core of highly persistent delinquents with repeated convictions' (the 'nutters', to use youth's own term), and he still accounts for them in psycho-dynamic terms, by reference to emotional development and family history.

West, in other words, redraws the line between morally normal and morally subnormal youth. Subnormality, at least for boys, is no longer equated with **a** criminal conviction but with **persistent** criminal convictions. (I'll discuss the implication that all **girl** delinquents **are** abnormal later.)

Explaining Juvenile Delinquency – The Sociological Approach

The psycho-dynamic approach to delinquency leaves a number of sociological questions unanswered. How can we explain the **normality** of delinquency for some young people in some places? Where do delinquent norms come from? How should we explain the **collective** aspect of youth crime? What is the significance of the gang? Why does delinquent behaviour take the **form** it does? What does it **mean** to the delinquents themselves? People don't have emotional urges to break milk bottles or go for joy-rides – these are **cultural** events.

American sociologists began the detailed study of delinquent **culture** in the 1920s. They argued that the psycho-dynamic approach was too negative, explained delinquency by reference to what **hadn't** happened, to the **lack** of healthy socialisation. The way forward theoretically was to look at what **had** happened, to discover how some young people **learnt** to be delinquent. Thus the criminologist **Edwin Sutherland** developed the theory of **differential association**. He argued that criminal behaviour is learnt and that the learning of criminal skills and values occurs primarily within 'intimate personal groups'. To become criminal, then, young people must value their associations with criminal groups more than their associations with non-criminal groups. Sutherland's point was that the choice of delinquent behaviour depended as much on the available patterns of social life as on people's 'dispositions'.

The 'Chicago School' of Sociology (based in Chicago University) elaborated this 'sub-cultural' approach to delinquency in a series of detailed studies of delinquents' social settings. One strategy was to analyse the delinquent group itself, **the gang**, describing its social organisation, its rules, its methods of recruitment, its power structure. To understand how delinquent gangs worked was to understand their appeal, their **function** for their members. This enabled social workers to develop their own boys' clubs and youth clubs as legitimate ways of fulfilling the same functions. Another group of researchers developed a broader **ethnography**, analysing the local and ethnic communities in which Chicago's youth gangs were based, tracing their patterns of socialisation so that delinquent **sub-cultures** could be related to the particular shape of their **parent cultures**.

These 1930s approaches were developed theoretically after the Second World War and I'll outline them in more detail in the next section. First I need to mention the most important pre-war 'cultural' account of delinquency, which came not from Chicago but derived from the work of the nineteenth century French sociologist, Emile Durkheim – **Robert Merton** applied Durkheim's concept of 'anomie' (normlessness) to American crime patterns and, in doing so, suggested an approach to youth crime that was to be extremely influential. The rising crime rate in the USA in the 1930s was the result, Merton argued, of an increasing disjunction between the American ideal of the equality of opportunity, the American definition of success in terms of material wealth and power, and the Depression reality of poverty and material failure, of 'blocked access' to educational and business opportunities for most lower class Americans.

Crime, Merton argued, signalled not the **rejection** of dominant American goals, but the adoption of **illegitimate means** to the pursuit of those goals. Juvenile delinquency, from this perspective, was thus best understood as reflecting a **confusion** about norms, about the relation of legitimate and illegitimate means and ends. Such 'anomie' had to be understood in terms of the wider society rather than by reference to inadequate socialisation within the family. The solution to delinquency, in other words, lay in economic and social change rather than in moral reform.

Gang Cultures and Street Corner Societies

The importance of Merton's work was to define delinquency as a problem of society, not the individual. It followed that the 'normality' or 'abnormality' of delinquents needed a socio-historical rather than a psychological explanation. Merton, though, like other pre-war sociologists, treated juvenile delinquency as the first move into a life of adult crime, and so reinforced the tendency to treat juvenile gangs as criminal in the same sorts of way as adult gangs. Post-war sociologists changed this tendency.

A. K. Cohen's study of delinquent boys, for example, concludes that juvenile gang delinquency was essentially 'non-utilitarian'. Most gang activities did **not** involve the pursuit of material goals but were, rather, 'maliciously' destructive (i.e. violence against people and property) and enjoyed for their immediate excitement – youth gangs, for example, stole cars not to resell but simply for the fun of joy-riding and crashing them. Crimes were committed for the hell of it, because they gave gangs and individual members of gangs status and prestige. The pleasure taken in trouble making and law breaking for their own sakes suggested to Cohen that delinquent gangs deliberately **reversed** social norms. Young people, Cohen argued, did not join gangs and therefore become anti-social, but, rather, 'anti-social' people got together in gangs because only such small, autonomous groups could sustain anti-social norms and status.

The question then became, why were some young people anti-social to begin with? Cohen suggested that this was a 'reaction formation' to their institutional experiences: 'certain children are denied status in the respectable society because they cannot meet the criteria of the respectable status system. The delinquent sub-culture deals with these problems by providing criteria of status which these children **can** meet.' The roots of delinquency lie, then, in children's failures at school and work, in their lack of social achievement and prestige in 'respectable' terms.

Cohen took from W. F. Whyte's classic study, *Street Corner Society*, a division in lower class youth culture between **college boys** and **corner boys**. College boys sought middle class status using middle class norms – an **individualistic** stress on education, qualifications, respectability, marriage. Corner boys developed a **collective inversion** of middle class norms, a stress on immediate pleasures, on rough activities, on celebrations of toughness and excitement that offered no future rewards. This corner/college boy distinction clearly reflected the tension between street and school values in 1950s teenage life that I discussed in chapter 2, and Cohen's argument was not that all corner boys necessarily became delinquent, but that delinquency could only be understood by reference to corner boy society. The question became why, given their shared social environment, some working class boys conformed to and some rebelled against the middle class norm.

Where Do Delinquent Values Come From?

The flaw in Cohen's approach to delinquency was his equation of 'middle class values' with the American norm – non-middle class values were therefore deviant, non-respectable, by definition. What this left out of account was the relationship of the corner boys to **working class values** (Cohen, like previous sociologists, assumed that juvenile delinquency was primarily a working class phenomenon).

This point was taken up by **Walter Miller**, who argued that young delinquents were best understood not in terms of their inversion of middle class values but as **conforming** to the norms of their 'lower class milieu'. What made them delinquent was not their 'deviant norms' but the **intensity** of their concern to conform to such lower class values as toughness and excitement and the resulting **conflicts** with middle class authority (in school, for example). The problem facing the corner boys, according to Miller, was not their failure in middle class terms but their **marginality**, as youth, in their local working class community. Young delinquents certainly resented having to engage with middle class authority, but their experiences at school and work were less important than their feelings of insignificance among their immediate neighbours and friends. And this milieu, Miller suggested, treats delinquency with tolerance and even respect. 'Getting into trouble' is accepted as a normal hazard of growing up working class and can, indeed, be a source of local prestige.

The flaw in Miller's approach was that it implied that **all** working class boys should be delinquent – it couldn't explain working class 'college boys' who were **deviant** in their cultural milieu. Subsequent studies have tried to address this issue, to explain different youth responses to the same cultural environment. **Cloward and Ohlin**, for example, suggested that working class teenagers have available a variety of ways of dealing with their marginal status – even the term 'delinquent' covers quite different sorts of behaviour. Whether people get involved in thieving, fighting or drug-taking depends, in part, on available **opportunities**. Young people don't make a firm, clear decision either to be a delinquent or a non-delinquent (to be a corner or a college boy), but, rather, respond to opportunities, find themselves engaged in particular sorts of conflict with various forms of authority. And what the authorities do (police and parents, courts and teachers) is as important in the production of 'delinquency' as what young people do.

David Matza developed this point by studying young people's own accounts of their activities. He discovered that they did not make any clear distinction between their 'delinquent' and 'non-delinquent' behaviour. Delinquents justified their 'deviant' acts by reference to the same 'respectable' norms which organised the rest of their lives. Delinquent acts occurred because the 'delinquents' believed that in certain circumstances 'normal' judgements could be suspended – to use a British example, skinheads justify 'Paki-bashing' and 'queer-bashing' by **excluding** Asians and gays from the community in which, as the skinheads themselves agree, hitting people for no reason is wrong. Matza concluded that 'becoming deviant' involves learning not deviant values but deviant **justifications**. As Sykes and Matza put it: 'It is our argument that much delinquency is based on what is essentially an unrecognised extension of **defences** to crimes in the form of justifications for deviance that are seen as valid by the delinquent but not by the legal system or society at large.' Hence the familiar excuses offered by young delinquents on arrest and in court – 'we didn't really hurt anybody', 'everyone else was doing it', 'the police started it'.

In his later work, Matza argued that just as deviants have their own sort of commitment to conformist values, so conformists have their own sort of commitment to deviant values. 1950s and 1960s USA had a **subterranean** as well as a dominant value system, a shared if furtive commitment to personal violence, non-conformity, rule-breaking and sexual adventure. Subterranean values are expressed through fantasy (all those Clint Eastwood films, for example) or in carefully demarcated times and places (on holidays, on the sports field, in red light districts), and what juvenile delinquents do wrong is bring subterranean norms to the social surface, acting out violent fantasies in real gang activities, being destructive and disorderly daily on the streets.

Explaining Juvenile Delinquency – Labelling Theory

Matza's argument made clear that 'delinquency' is the result of the **interaction** of people behaving in certain ways and other people responding to that behaviour. To call an **action** delinquent is also to describe the social **reaction** to it. This approach to deviance, as developed by **Howard Becker** and his colleagues, is known as 'labelling theory' although, as Becker argues, it should be called **the interactionist theory of deviance**.

It's a theory which raises a number of important points. First, labelling theorists explain delinquency as a **process** (not a state). What sociologists have to make sense of are situations in which delinquency may or may not be constructed – not every football match leads to 'trouble', not every football hooligan gets into a fight. Reactions by the police and passers-by and the media are as important for the occurrence of 'delinquency' as actions by delinquents. Delinquency is often experienced therefore as accidental, a matter of chance not choice – which both adds to the excitement of delinquent occasions and explains why young people feel so aggrieved when they are confronted – 'why pick on **me**?'

It follows too that if action and reaction are equally significant for the making of delinquency then they should be paid the same amount of sociological attention. Becker and his colleagues were thus able to show how **deviancy amplification** works: being labelled as a deviant can intensify someone's commitment to deviancy. The most obvious British example of this process is the police labelling of black youth – by treating black teenagers as 'trouble' just because of the 'deviant' colour of their skins, policemen both encourage and legitimate the black youth rejection of 'white' law and order.

Labelling theory, then, has changed sociologists' ideas about **who** should be studied in the analysis of delinquency – the labellers need as much study as the labelled. We must, for example, be able to explain the **moral entrepreneurs** (the newspaper writers and moralists and political speech makers) who defined the 'problems' of teddy boys and punks and Hell's Angels, dope smoking and glue sniffing, football hooliganism and mugging. The labels applied to delinquents have their own sociological, historical and cultural meanings – why have they developed the way they have? To go back to the beginning of the chapter, why have people thought for so long that hooliganism is a 'new' problem, that young people were once well behaved?

These questions became particularly important for sociologists in the 1960s when some youth deviants claimed a political justification for their deviance, when the moral certainties of the labellers were put into doubt. Thus, in his influential study of the mods and rockers phenomenon, **Stanley Cohen** focused on press, political and court **responses** to the seaside battles. He was interested in how 'moral panics' worked. And, in general, sociologists now include discussion of police and media behaviour in studies of juvenile delinquency as a matter of course – even Lord Scarman's report on the 1981 'riots' paid attention to police and press contributions to the trouble.

Female Delinquency

I'll return to the general implications of labelling theory for the sociology of youth in chapter 5. Here I want to draw attention to some of the gaps and weaknesses of delinquency theory itself.

Most obviously and most seriously, 'delinquency' studies have focused almost exclusively on **male** behaviour. Sociologists have accepted the statistical indications that delinquency is an aspect of growing up male (about ten boys appear in court for every one girl) without considering what they really mean. Are such statistics the best measure of 'delinquency'? Isn't labelling theory relevant here? Policemen faced with a football crowd, for example, are more likely to pick on boys as the trouble makers, to tell the girls to go home, so maybe girls' absence from the courts the next week tells us more about police attitudes to women than about girls' attitudes to crime.

Even if girls aren't as delinquent as boys (or are delinquent in different ways) we still need to be able to account for such differences, and it's not clear that existing sociological approaches can. After all, girls also experience blocked access to material rewards, they too fail at school, have a marginal status in the community. And girls also become punks and skinheads, share lower class and subterranean values. So why don't delinquency theories discuss them? None of the theories I have summarised presents itself as an explicitly **gendered** explanation of delinquency; the theorists refer to class rather than to male values. The fact is that male sociologists have, on the whole, shared the attitude of police and courts that female delinquency is unusual. This statistical conclusion conceals a theoretical assumption, as feminist sociologists have more recently pointed out – girls can't be brought into sociological accounts of delinquency and so explanations of their behaviour can be left to the social psychologists. Thus D. J. West's *The Young Offenders* moves from the finding that girls are far less delinquent than boys to the conclusion that girls who are delinquent are **abnormal** – their behaviour has to be explained in psycho-dynamic rather than cultural terms. West notes that 'wayward girls are worse than delinquent boys', are more likely to come from 'disordered' homes, to show 'neurotic symptoms' and 'psychopathic traits'. But the most significant aspect of West's conclusions is that they relate female delinquency to **sexual** misbehaviour: 'girl thieves are often, but not always, sexual rebels'. Other criminologists have taken this suggestion even further. Cowie, Cowie and Slater's 1968 survey, *Delinquency in Girls*, for example, linked female delinquency to abnormal 'hormonal balance' – 'sex chromosome constitution is one of the basic factors determining the liability to delinquency'.

This is to return explanations of delinquency to nineteenth century assumptions, and it is a measure of the inadequacy of sociological accounts of delinquency that such a biological approach still had credibility at the end of the 1960s. Two points about this should be stressed, in particular. First, the idea that female delinquency is 'abnormal' and likely to be linked to sexual activity has material consequences for the girls who are brought to court. They are more likely than boys to be declared 'in need of care, protection or control', more likely to be given custodial sentences, even if these sentences are passed 'for their own good'. As Cowie, Cowie and Slater explain magistrates' actions: 'these girls have to be removed from society into the security of a residential school much more for their own sakes than to protect society'.

Second, there is an obvious double standard at work here: girls' sexual activity is treated as 'problematic' in a way that boys' sexual activity is not (boy shop-lifters who come to court are not usually questioned about their sex lives). This double standard is not just applied by courts and criminologists; within youth cultures themselves female behaviour is judged differently than male behaviour; girls are labelled by boys on the streets (as 'slags' or 'drags', for example) as well as by police and social workers in court reports. Sexual assumptions and gender divisions are built into youth sub-cultures, and the real problem of delinquency theory is not that it ignores female delinquency, but that in doing so it provides only a partial and inadequate account of male behaviour. I'll return to this point in chapter 6.

Race and Crime

Black youth has become a 'problem' in Britain in the last twenty years, in much the same way that white working class youth became a 'problem' in the nineteenth century. The sight of male teenagers hanging around public places in groups, dressed in distinctive clothes, 'doing nothing' and getting into trouble triggers off press and police suspicions now as it did a hundred years ago – then the youth problem was labelled 'hooliganism'; in the late 1960s the black youth problem became encapsulated in the headlines about 'mugging'.

In the most important sociological study of youth, race and crime, *Policing The Crisis*, Stuart Hall and his colleagues show how mugging (meaning robbery from a person in a public place involving assault or the threat of assault) was a label developed to refer to more general fears about **law and order** and about **race relations**. Mugging is not a legal category ('muggers' are actually charged with a variety of robbery or assault offences) but it does carry a common sense meaning. It describes, for example, an offence that is seen to be essentially **irrational**. Mugging means random violence, an attack that could be experienced by any law abiding citizen. Mugging, unlike vandalism, may have a material 'reason' – it is a form of theft – but press reports concentrate on its most pointless examples: 'Pensioner Beaten For Fourpence!' And mugging is a crime that is seen to make particular **places** dangerous – areas of cities, tube stations, underpasses. In the headlines, then, mugging stands for a **breakdown** of law and order – in certain places, in particular communities.

This relates to the second aspect of mugging as a label: its association with **race**. The places and people linked to mugging become the places and people linked to certain sorts of social change, certain sorts of 'strangeness' – people and places linked, that is, to 'immigration' and 'immigrants'. By the 1970s black muggers had become the symbol (in both Britain and the USA) of white fears (made public by racist organisations like the National Front) of black neighbours and black neighbourhoods. Hall and his colleagues conclude that we can't understand the 'problem' of black youth without understanding the political and cultural activities of white adults.

There are several sociological studies now showing how this sort of labelling affected policing and sentencing, how black youth culture was 'criminalised' (this is, as I have suggested, a clear case of 'deviancy amplification'). Other researchers have examined the crime statistics themselves, showing that mugging is not a very serious problem (people are far more likely to be burgled than mugged), that the young are more likely than the old to be attacked, that racial identities of muggers and victims fall into no neat patterns. But, as *Policing The Crisis* suggests, while it is important for sociologists to replace the myth of mugging with rational analysis, this should not be done by ignoring black youth culture altogether. Nineteenth century 'hooliganism' was a myth too, but the label did refer to something of the shifting experience of working class boys in the big cities, and the mugging label too refers to a real aspect of black youth culture, its **street** presence, its organisation of black Britons from West Indian family backgrounds around certain sorts of leisure **style**.

Sociological arguments about black youth culture draw on the theories developed to make sense of white youth sub-cultures, relating their developments to boys' failures and lack of status in middle class institutions, to the rejection of middle class values, to the celebration of subterranean norms. The difference between black and white youth cultures is that black youth have to deal not simply with 'middle class' values, but with **white** middle class values. School failure involves a discrediting of black culture and language; work failure involves racial discrimination. For black youth, too, a job is not necessarily a desirable mark of adult status; it may involve commitment to an apparent lifetime of subservience to white authority. Hall and his colleagues argue that this has two consequences. First, black youth culture has a tendency to forms of cultural **nationalism** – middle class norms are rejected via an assertion of pride in black identity. Second, black youth culture involves, more clearly than white youth culture, a rejection of a simple work ethic, a stress on self-employment, on 'hustling' as a means of getting by. Black youth, in short, use local streets and other public places as the setting for work as well as leisure, politics as well as pleasure. It is not surprising that they get associated with 'street crimes' like mugging, that they come into conflict with the police – the conflict that lay behind the 1981 'riots'.

Explaining Juvenile Delinquency – Begged Questions and Unresolved Issues

One of the complaints facing sociologists is that in seeking to **explain** behaviour, they are actually trying to **justify** it. This is a particularly vigorous complaint about the sociology of deviance and delinquency: sociologists, by the very nature of their work, are thought to be 'on the side of the criminals'. This is, in practice, a matter of sociologists' individual political and ethical positions. A more important sociological problem, it seems to me, is that in developing general explanations of why some young people **are** delinquent, sociologists are in danger of leaving it unclear why most young people **are not**. In focusing on 'problem youth' sociologists have contributed to the idea that young people are, in themselves, 'a problem'. I have already suggested that this means ignoring girls, who don't fit the various deviancy models (so that accounts of black youth culture too leave it unclear whether there are female muggers, what their behaviour means), and it has other obvious consequences – Asian youth are neglected in the literature, for example, they are not 'problems' in the right sort of way.

At the beginning of this chapter I cited Geoffrey Pearson's study of the 'respectable fears' adults have had of youth for at least a hundred years. Why have adults so consistently 'over-reacted' to juvenile delinquency? Why does reasonable concern about teenage bad behaviour so often take on the exaggerated form of a 'moral panic'? Stanley Cohen suggests that moral panics reflect adult attempts to cope with certain sorts of social change, to deal with anxiety about a society's economic or moral stability. Young people become the target for such anxiety because they are highly visible (their leisure behaviour is on public display) and relatively powerless (the forces of moral order, police and social workers, teachers and courts can do things to them, can be seen to **act**).

The 'problem' of youthful deviancy is, thus, in many ways, a projection on to the young of adult concerns, and this goes too, for the sociology of youthful deviancy. Sociologists have also slipped from explanations of specific delinquents into the suggestion that all young people are deviant, have begged the question of the relationship between deviancy and conformity, between growing up working class, or male or black and growing up 'normal'. And sociologists too have projected on to youth their own political concerns. This is particularly the case with British sub-cultural theory, which I will discuss in the next two chapters.

Chapter Five

Sub-cultural Theory

Youth Groups in Britain

Passers-by were first startled (and frightened) by the Edwardian cow-
boy look of the Teddy Boys in the early 1950s, and ever since then
British youth cultures have been associated in the public's mind with
bizarre street styles. The Teds were followed in the 1960s by Mods and
Rockers, in the 1970s by Skinheads and Punks. Youth styles change but
rarely vanish. Saturday afternoon shopping in most provincial towns
still means watching a spectacular parade of the main youth styles of
the last thirty years (not to mention the more specialist displays of the
Rockabillies and Bowie Boys, the Heavy Metal Kids and Soulies, the
New Mods and Ois).

Such youthful identity is a matter of looking right (clothes, shoes,
hairstyles) and sharing tastes (for styles of music, ways of having fun),
and however different such youth groups are from each other (differences which have sometimes involved ritual fights – mods vs rockers,
teds vs punks) they equally outrage 'straight' society – grown-ups, shop
keepers, the police, teachers, newspapers quick to use such peculiar
images (girls with rings in their noses, boys with tattooed heads) for
their shock value. In Britain the general fears about young people –
what are our children coming to? – have been focused on the public
eccentricities of working class youth styles. The sociological question
is: what do these styles **mean**?

The sociological answer to this question rests on the concept of 'sub-
culture'. In dictionary terms, a sub-culture is 'a social, ethnic or
economic group with a particular character of its own **within** a culture
or society', and this was how the term was first used by sociologists – to
draw attention to the distinctive cultural patterns of minority groups

within 'plural' societies (thus we might talk of Mormon sub-culture in the USA or Chinese sub-culture in Britain).

At first glance British youth groups, however distinctive their look, don't fit this model. Young people of all styles are still defined by the dominant cultural institutions of family and school, class and work place; their styles are not ways of life but aspects of leisure. On the other hand, these leisure groups (which seem to be a uniquely British phenomenon) can't be accounted for in terms of other theories of youth either. They're 'deviant' but not necessarily delinquent – it's not a **crime** to dye your hair green. Their styles depend on commercial teen culture (pop music most obviously) but weren't created by it – ted and mod and punk and skinhead styles certainly weren't dreamed up by businessmen. The young people involved aren't 'classless' – they seem to be working class in social origin and setting – but neither are they obviously embedded in their parent cultures. British youth styles appear as bizarre in their local communities of family and neighbours as they do to middle class and media observers. Sub-culture does seem an appropriate term to get at these youth groups' sense of **difference** from society, as long as we continue to be clear that youth sub-cultures are, at the same time, embedded **in** society.

Sociologists developed the sub-cultural theory of youth, then, to show how young working class 'deviance' is, in fact, an effect of dominant cultural patterns. In the words of *Resistance Through Rituals*, the classic study of youth style published in 1975:

> We have tried to dismantle the term in which this subject is usually discussed – 'Youth Culture' – and reconstruct in its place a more careful picture of the kinds of youth sub-cultures, their relation to class cultures and to the way cultural hegemony [domination] is maintained structurally and historically.

The Origins of Sub-cultural Theory

As this quote from *Resistance Through Rituals* makes clear, the sub-cultural approach to youth is not easily summarised. It marked a new perspective on youth culture, but one which wove together strands of other approaches, and developed a particularly opaque theoretical jargon. In this chapter I will try to provide a 'simple' account of sub-cultural theory while using direct quotations to give an idea of the woolliness of much of the finished product. The most useful starting point is the American delinquency theory discussed in the last chapter. The aim of the Chicago School in the 1920s and 1930s was to outline a sociological alternative to criminologists' positivist accounts of delinquent behaviour, to provide social rather than individual explanations of juvenile crime. The empirical basis of this was ethnography, detailed observation and description of teenage gangs, which attempted to get at the group values which justified individual delinquent acts. The argument was that, in its cultural context, delinquency was 'normal', determined by cultural norms, and not a symptom of psychological deficiency. Even apparently 'non-rational' delinquent behaviour (like vandalism or street fighting) could be understood from this perspective. It might not bring material benefits (like robbery) but it did win status and prestige according to gang values of risk and toughness. The Chicago sociologists understood juvenile delinquency as **collective** behaviour organised around gangs' 'focal values'. Youth deviance had to be explained, in short, in terms of young people's membership of delinquent sub-cultures, and the question became where did these sub-cultures' values come from? How did they relate to the USA's dominant value system?

Over the last fifty years American sociologists have come up with various answers to this question. The most important were outlined in the last chapter:

a) delinquency is the result of blocked access to social rewards, both material (wealth and power) and cultural (status and prestige). Sub-cultures are deviant not in their ends but in their means to those ends (Merton).
b) delinquents deliberately reverse dominant social values in order to legitimate and cope with their 'failure' according to those values (A. K. Cohen).
c) delinquency is an aspect of 'lower-class culture' – it is deviant only according to middle class norms (Miller).
d) delinquency involves the 'inappropriate expression' of widely shared but 'subterranean' social values (Matza).
e) deviance is an effect of labelling – youth groups are 'delinquent' because of the reactions to them by societies' moral authorities (teachers, police, courts, social workers, mass media) (Becker).

Each of these arguments was developed in response to the explanatory weaknesses of the others, and British sub-cultural theorists too began by taking what they could from these positions to make sense of the history of British youth cultures. The general sociological tasks were the same: to explain deviant behaviour by reference to sub-cultural values, to show that the most irrational styles (shaved heads, ripped clothes) were 'normal', to tease out the relationship between sub-cultures and society. What British theorists added to the argument was a Marxist perspective. American youth theorists were concerned with the social production of norms in the immediate circumstances of collective behaviour (in gangs and on street corners) and with the relationship of 'deviant' and 'normal' values but didn't pay much attention to where these norms came from. British youth theorists wanted to develop a wider social structural perspective. Influenced in part by the emergence of a Marxist 'new criminology' in the late 1960s, which related crime to the **class** structure, they sought to link youthful deviance too to class **conflict**.

Youth and Class Conflict

British sociologists of youth (like their American counterparts) are agreed that deviant youth sub-cultures are working class sub-cultures. The young people concerned come from working class families and neighbourhoods, have a working class experience of growing up – they're in the lower streams at school, leave as soon as possible to look for a job, they're unemployed or passing through a succession of dead end tasks and training schemes. The sociological questions follow from these empirical observations: what is the relationship between such young people's class-based experiences and their sub-cultural styles? How do deviant groups express **working class** 'values'? What is their connection to working class parent culture? Why are such styles adopted by only a minority of working class youngsters? Are the Teds and Mods, the Punks and Skinheads, more or less 'class conscious' than their 'normal' peers?

British sub-cultural theory began from the answer to this last question. Deviant styles are, obviously, non-conformist and such non-conformity is, according to *Resistance Through Rituals*, not simply a gesture of adolescent rebellion against parents but involves, more importantly, a confrontation with middle class authorities, a statement of working class identity. A skinhead gang is an 'us' against 'them' gesture writ large in class rather than generational terms. The shock value of deviant styles, their effect in making people jump, getting boys and girls sent home from school, turned down from jobs, picked on by the police, is essential to their meaning. Young people in the late 1970s, for example, didn't just dye their hair green because they liked the colour, but also because they knew what effect this would have on other people. They wanted to **parade** their rebellion, and this was a rebellion not against working class experiences as such but against middle class attempts to define and confine those experiences.

American sociologists like Miller had argued that young delinquents expressed lower class culture 'naturally' – they articulated in intense and public but spontaneous ways the beliefs and values they had grown up with (notions of masculinity, what it means to be a 'real man', in particular). British sub-cultural writers developed this argument with the suggestion that deviant stylists weren't simply reflecting, unconsciously, existing working class norms (though macho values were an obvious part of British youth cultures too) but using them as the basis of a form of **resistance** to the expectations of school and leisure and workplace. It is their visible, public, **collective** commitment to such resistance that differentiates these youth groups **both** from conforming 'normal' working class youngsters **and** from A. K. Cohen's 'corner boys'. The latter may 'reverse' bourgeois norms in order to generate immediate social status from their 'failure' but they're not concerned to **symbolise** their position, to publicise their revolt by turning it into a public style.

Resistance Through Rituals

To define sub-cultural style as 'working class resistance' is to make two sociological assertions: first, that the style relates to specifically working class experiences (and not just to general adolescent concerns for fashion and peer group solidarity) and, second, that the style is a 'political' response to those experiences, works, that is, to give the stylists some sort of power over their situation, a way of confronting authority. Neither claim rings immediately true in common sense terms, if only because the various youth uniforms, in their very precision, seem so 'irrational'. The Marxist New Criminologists linked crime to class via a straightforwardly materialistic argument. To put it crudely, if you're in a low paid job or unemployed, with no prospects or qualifications, then robbery is an obvious way of making money and gaining social status. But what does putting on crepe soles or having a mohican haircut achieve? If the underlying cause of deviance is young people's class position, their relationship to the means of economic production, then why do styles change (when material conditions don't)? Why did people become Teds in the 1950s, Mods in the 1960s, Punks in the 1970s? What does it mean to choose to become a Skinhead rather than a Rocker?

What's at issue in such choices is not a change in material circumstances but a use of symbols, and in trying to explain how **symbolic behaviour** was a form of class resistance sub-cultural writers drew their arguments directly from labelling theory. Labelling theorists had argued that social deviance is an effect of the activities of labellers, but left it rather unclear why the labellers, the moral entrepreneurs in society, acted the way they did. American labelling theory, in particular, was essentially pluralistic in its assumptions. It described society in terms of a value competition in which the labellers (because of their social position) had the power to make their labels stick, while the labelled, low status minority groups, hadn't. Sub-culturalist theorists rejected this idea of a free competition of ideas and argued, instead, that 'labellers', particularly as they are organised in state institutions (the police force, schools, the law, the social services), are the bearers of **bourgeois** values. They don't just happen to have different attitudes from deviants; their values (and the labelling process itself) derive from the problems of maintaining an orderly capitalist society.

The difference between the pluralist and Marxist use of labelling theory is clear from a comparison of Stan Cohen's account of the media responses to mods and rockers, which he describes in terms of a 'moral panic', something essentially irrational, and Stuart Hall and his colleagues' analysis of the media responses to mugging, which they related to a **political** crisis such that problems of law and order and race couldn't be separated from an analysis of class relations (see the discussion of these books in chapter 4). The point to be taken from the latter argument is that disputes about youth styles (and mugging as a social issue, as I've already suggested, raised the particular problem of black youth style) are **real** disputes. There may be no obvious material stakes (as in a strike over wages) when skinheads are sent home from school or banned from football grounds, when the police stop and question anyone with dreadlocks, but such confrontations do concern the way in which the social structure is 'reproduced'. What's going on, from this theoretical perspective, is **class struggle at the ideological level** (and in 1981 no-one could deny that the youth 'riots' in Brixton, Toxteth and Bristol were **political** events).

Resistance and Ideology

The crucial distinction between American delinquency theory and British sub-cultural theory lies in the latter's use of the concept of ideology. Both approaches agree that deviant behaviour is best understood as a form of problem solving. In Mike Brake's words, 'sub-cultures arise as attempts to resolve collectively experienced problems arising from contradictions in the social structure'. Working class youth are in a marginal position in contemporary capitalist societies. They lack power, status and wealth now, and they already know that they will have extremely limited access to power, status and wealth in the future. Youth deviance is thus a way of generating alternative forms of success and reward. This was the great insight of American sociology, and British writers' problem was to apply it to deviant styles.

In what way do they **solve** youth problems? Skinheads still lack power and property however short their hair and frightening their appearance, and the argument became, then, that deviant styles are solutions to ideological problems, a response to the gaps and contradictions in the set of **ideas** that young people are offered (by parents, by the media, by the teenage consumption industry, by the state) as a way of **making sense of their marginality.**

If we want to explain the emergence of skinheads in the late 1960s, in other words, we should examine not their material conditions (experiences at home and work didn't change much in this period) but their cultural conditions; we should analyse the available ways of interpreting the world. Youth sub-cultures solve ideological problems and to make sociological sense of them we must begin by understanding their 'ideological conditions of existence'. Thus *Resistance Through Rituals* provides a history of British youth groups not in terms of wages or job opportunities or educational organisation but in terms of changing **ideas** about youth and leisure and style. Phil Cohen summed up this approach in his pioneering study of skinheads:

> the latent function of sub-culture is this – to express and resolve, albeit 'magically', the contradictions which appear in the parent culture. The succession of sub-cultures which this parent culture generated can thus all be considered as so many variations on a central theme – the contradiction, at an ideological level, between traditional working class puritanism and the new ideology of consumption . . .

For Cohen, then, the 'problem' facing young people in Britain since the war had been to make sense of competing systems of meaning and morality – traditional working class emphasis on the importance of workplace solidarity, community and family life, middle class emphasis on educational opportunity and individual ambition, media emphasis on consumption and fun. The 'magical' solution was to develop a style, a form of group leisure that negotiated a path between such competing values by presenting individual prestige in terms of collective consumption. Cohen suggested that sub-cultures should be seen as **ritual** solutions to cultural contradictions, and the question became how such rituals worked as forms of 'resistance'.

The Concept of Hegemony

The argument of 'resistance through rituals' rests on the concept of **hegemony**, which was first developed by the Italian Marxist, Antonio Gramsci, in the 1920s. Hegemony means leadership or domination, and Gramsci's purpose in using the term was to draw attention to the role of cultural institutions (the church, the family, the law, education, the arts, the media) in the organisation of power in class societies. He argued that the bourgeoisie in capitalist societies is the ruling class (is 'hegemonic') not just because it controls the 'repressive' state forces (the police and military) and owns the means of economic production, but also because it dominates the 'civil institutions', the way people organise their 'private' lives and their 'common sense', the ways in which they each understand their situation, decide what's right or wrong, possible or impossible, natural or unnatural. To be 'hegemonic' a class has to impose its ideology, its particular organisation of values, beliefs and symbols, on everyone else, and class conflict thus involves a struggle for ideas as well as a struggle for state power and economic resources. It follows that ideological resistance is a key form of political activity – all challenges to a ruling class depend on people who are convinced that society could be organised otherwise, that present social arrangements aren't 'necessary' or 'natural'.

Deviant youth styles are a real threat to the ruling class, then, because they challenge dominant **ideas** – which is why they provoke 'panics'. And even struggles over ideas have material effects. In the words of *Resistance Through Rituals*:

> sub-cultures are not simply 'ideological' constructs. They, too, **win space** for the young: cultural space in the neighbourhood and institutions, real time for leisure and recreation, actual room on the street or street-corner. They serve to mark out and appropriate 'territory' in the localities. They focus around key occasions of social interaction: the weekend, the disco, the bank-holiday trip, the night-out in the 'centre', and 'stand-about-doing-nothing' of the weekday evening, the Saturday match.

Sub-cultures and Style

I think anybody reading this description will be struck by the gap between the sociologists' abstract account of youth sub-culture and the explanations for their behaviour one would be likely to get from the sub-cultures themselves. Punks and Skinheads and Mods and Teds are unlikely (unless they've done Sociology A-Level) to talk about 'winning cultural space', 'resistance at the ideological level' or the 'magical reclamation of community', and an obvious comment to be made on sub-cultural theory is that it reads into youth styles meanings that aren't there. There has always been a tendency for sociologists (who usually come from middle class, bookish backgrounds) to celebrate teenage deviancy, to admire the loyalties and excitement of 'street life', to forget the painful problems that cause street life to be like that in the first place. If for American delinquency theorists this meant romanticising gang life, have Marxist sub-cultural theorists romanticised 'resistance'?

This is an aspect of youth culture – the way it is used by other people, sociologists included, to symbolise certain values, to carry certain messages – that I'll come back to. The sub-cultural theorists themselves, while acknowledging that their conclusions don't derive from questionnaires or interviews, claim, nevertheless, to be using an objective approach. Their interpretations of sub-cultural styles are ordered by **semiology**, the science of signs. Theorists have drawn particularly on the work of the French semiologist, Roland Barthes, whose work was full of suggestive comments about the ways 'signs' work in everyday life. The significance of people's clothes, the meanings of advertisements, the implications of the names and shapes of, say, motor-cars, are all socially constructed even if we normally take them for granted. How such images work depends on their organisation of cultural elements whose resonance comes from their meanings in other settings, from their contrast to 'opposing' signs. Thus a skinhead's short hair takes part of its meaning from other images of short hair (on a Borstal boy or army recruit), part from its opposition to long hair (on a hippie). Sub-cultural styles in general depend for their effect on 'bricolage', the accumulation in one uniform of signs taken from all sorts of context (the union jack moved from the flag-pole to a skinhead T-shirt, the swastika moved from a nazi uniform to a punk ear-lobe, and so on). Youth sub-cultures **take-over** signs – from respectable society (the mods' suits and ties), from disreputable society (the punks' bondage gear), above all from commercial teenage culture, and reassemble them in images which shock not just because they are unusual but because they also threaten the usual stability of imagery. Think, for example, of people's unease, anger even, at seeing boys with long hair and 'dresses' (hippies in the 1960s or Boy George followers in the 1980s) and girls (skinheads, punks, feminists) with short hair and 'masculine' work clothes. Such deviant use of clothing becomes a challenge to dominant conventions of sexuality.

According to sub-cultural theory, then, youth styles are a form of resistance not because the stylists are consciously challenging 'bourgeois ideology' but because in using social signs to give themselves a sense of control over their own lives, group members simultaneously draw public attention to the contradictions in the dominant ideology as it relates to their lives. In the words of *Resistance Through Rituals*, 'the Teddy Boy expropriation of an upper class style of dress "covered" the gap between largely manual, unskilled, near-lumpen real careers and life-chances, and the "all-dressed-up-and-nowhere-to-go" experience of Saturday evening', while 'in the expropriation and fetishisation of consumption and style itself, the Mods covered the gap between the never-ending-weekend and Monday's resumption of boring, dead-end work'.

Sub-cultural Theory: Does It Make Sense

We can summarise the sub-cultural argument like this, then. Youth groups use their own area of power – their 'free time' – to make a gesture against their lot. Their material situation (school failure, unemployment, no future), is, at one level, accepted – there is nothing they can do about it – but, at another level, rejected – deviant styles symbolise a refusal to accept dominant accounts of their position. Youth sub-cultures can only cast spells against the boring powerlessness of the daily routine, but such magic does have cultural consequences. It challenges the ideology that normally keeps the social machinery working.

The sub-cultural approach to youth culture is complex, sometimes confused, and overtly Marxist but it has become, nonetheless, a central strand in the British sociology of youth. All other theorists have had to take account of it and the next chapter will examine their responses. A final point needs to be made here, though.

Sub-cultural theory rests on remarkably limited empirical research. The readings of youth styles in *Resistance Through Rituals*, for example, are based not on direct observation but on media sources – youth styles are analysed according to the ways they've **already** been labelled. This gives the description of style as conflict a certain conviction – the media do set up sub-cultures as 'threats' to society – but it also raises doubts about the real extent of those threats. In the two important empirical studies that have emerged from the sub-cultural school the doubts become pressing. Thus Paul Willis's *Learning To Labour* shows clearly enough that the 'lads' sub-culture is a form of resistance to schooling, but he also makes it plain that it exactly fits the lads for their future as workers, as unskilled manual labourers. Angela McRobbie's interviews with teenage girls show, similarly, that their 'feminine' style is both a form of resistance in the class room **and** a way of preparing themselves for their future roles as housewives, as domestic labourers.

The 'resistance' displayed by sub-cultures, in short, may be exaggerated by sociologists' concentration on the most spectacular aspects of youth culture (the aspects that interest the media). Willis and McRobbie, in placing such spectacle in its 'ordinary' context of work and leisure, school and family, make clear that the line between 'conforming' and 'non-conforming' youth is, in practice, hard to draw. If there are elements of resistance in sub-cultures, there are also elements of incorporation (and, indeed, some sub-cultures seem over-conformist to dominant norms, in their racial and sexual attitudes, for example). If youth cultures pose, in Dick Hebdige's words, 'an oblique challenge to hegemony', might they not also represent an equally oblique form of acquiescence to dominant social norms?

Chapter Six

Critiques of Sub-cultural Theory

The Feminist Critique

The most telling criticisms of sub-cultural theory concern its account of girls, or, rather, its lack of an account of girls. This point was made by Angela McRobbie and Jenny Garber in the *Resistance Through Rituals* collection itself. Why, they asked, were girls absent from the accompanying analyses of Teds and Mods and Skinheads? Were girls really absent from sub-cultures (and if so, why)? Or were they there but not noticed by sociologists (and if not, why not)? What was apparent was that in ignoring girls, sub-culturalists were ignoring boys' relationships with girls, were ignoring sub-cultural sexuality, the groups' attitudes to marriage and the family. Boys' 'masculinity' was taken for granted; 'resistance' was defined solely in terms of class and race; sub-cultures' political complicity with dominant sexual norms was not discussed.

Angela McRobbie has followed up these points in her subsequent research. Her empirical studies confirm that girls **are** members of sub-cultures but in marginal, 'feminine' positions that reflect the boys' 'normal' sexual expectations. Girls are defined as 'girl friends', for example. Female skinheads and punks are certainly rebelling against the mainstream culture of femininity, but within the sub-culture themselves traditional working class gender divisions still seem to hold.

McRobbie also suggests that there is not really such a thing as a **female sub-culture**, a way in which working class girls can resist dominant cultural norms collectively, as a group of girls. Young teenagers do share a 'teenybopper' or 'bedroom' culture, female friendship groups based on the home, on girls' magazines like *Jackie*, on pop stars and pin-ups, but these friendships become less significant as girls grow older, as their lives become defined by their marginal status in sub-cultures or by their incorporation into the commercial culture of femininity.

The implication of this sort of research is that the teenage activities analysed in sub-cultural theory, the activities that are described as 'resistance through rituals' or 'winning cultural space', are **male** activities. If girls do 'win space' or 'resist through rituals' they do so differently than boys, in ways that male sociologists haven't noticed. Why are there such differences between male and female teenage behaviour?

One still influential answer to this derives from the social-psychological approach to youth developed at the beginning of the century. This explains the cultural differences between boys and girls in biological terms. Girls are said to be 'naturally' passive, conformist and uninterested in joining groups. Puberty thus marks the onset of psychological as well as physical differences between the sexes. G. Stanley Hall's *Adolescence*, the source of this sort of argument, suggested that 'adolescence' actually meant quite different things for boys and girls. Adolescent boys became ambitious, curious, in need of mental growth and challenge; adolescent girls became emotional, prone to weepiness and giggling, flirtatious, in need of social protection as their maternal instincts emerged.

Such attempts to explain cultural norms in terms of hormones and instincts are no longer sociologically credible, but they do, to an unfortunate extent, still inform the common sense of parents and teachers, social workers and magistrates' courts. As I have already mentioned (see chapter 4), girls who do get involved in aggressive, gang activities are treated not as naughty but as abnormal. Female delinquency is still interpreted as the mark of a sexual problem; girls are still thought to be in special need of social protection.

The central feminist criticism of sub-cultural theory (particularly now that it is dominant in the British sociology of youth) is that in failing to account for the gender differences in youth culture, it has left common sense assumptions about sexuality unchallenged.

The Liberal Critique

The liberal critique of sub-cultural theory has been argued most passionately in Britain by David Marsland, who objects to the theory of 'resistance through rituals' because of its **Marxist** assumptions. I'm labelling Marsland's argument 'the liberal critique' (it's not his own term) because his underlying explanation of how British society does and should work is an essentially liberal position. He opposes the

Marxist model of classes in conflict with a liberal model of individuals pursuing and negotiating economic, social and moral freedom.

Marsland's liberal starting point has a number of implications for his sociology of youth. He rejects, for example, the sub-cultural suggestion that 'youth', as an explanatory concept, is meaningless, must be subordinated to the concept of class. The sub-culturalists argue that the activities and values of sixteen year-olds must be explained, in the end, by reference to their class position. The differences between growing up working class and growing up middle class are far more significant than the fact that members of the different classes all have to 'grow up'. Marsland retorts that youth culture does have some autonomy, refers to sets of beliefs that young members of all classes relate to. He suggests that in the explanation of why sixteen year-olds act and behave as they do, class is only one variable among many. Its relative importance can only be assessed empirically, will be different for different groups in different situations. As an age group, young people of all classes do share the structural problems of the transition from childhood to maturity; they are well aware of their difference from the other age groups in society.

Marsland's own conclusions from this are paradoxical. He begins by stressing how much cultural 'freedom' young people have (he's not willing, therefore, to interpret sub-cultural styles as **determined** by people's class position). Teenagers are relatively free of adult responsibility and control; they are institutionally separated from adults and have the market power to develop their own cultural symbols; they are in a strong position to **reject** adult norms and assumptions. Youth culture is, therefore, an expression of **autonomy**. But Marsland goes on to argue that precisely because teenagers are so free, adults have a duty to guide them. Sub-cultural theory suggests that official adult interference in youth cultures (via the Youth Service, for example) is a form of **social control**, an aspect of class struggle. Marsland argues that the Youth Service is necessary for young people's own good. He accepts that 'through the medium of youth culture young people are substantially involved in resistance and challenge to many of the fundamental features of modern society', but suggests that 'the Youth Service cannot allow themselves to collude in phony dreams'.

Marsland's overall approach to youth is best summarised in his own words: 'This freedom that they have is authentic, and at the same time terrible. For they must navigate its open seas without charts; live out a life in it without a structure of beliefs; be themselves while pursuing an identity without which they cannot yet be themselves at all; travelling here, since only here in leisure are they free, towards adulthood with only childhood to guide them; wishing for adult guidance and support and finding precious little. It is a painful privilege indeed, from any perspective, and from some perspectives manifestly a punishment rather than a privilege at all.'

I'm not sure that Marsland's arguments amount to a **theory** of youth, but they do, at least, remind us that while the problems of being young may be shaped **by** class position, they are not simply problems **of** class position. As the feminist critique also made clear, youth cultures are not **just** class cultures.

'Ordinary' Youth

Marsland's work makes a regular rhetorical appeal to the lives of 'ordinary' youth. The priority of the Youth Services he suggests, for example, should be 'the ordinary problems of ordinary young people of all social types in their transition out of childhood into adulthood'. He neglects, though, the most detailed sociological accounts of such ordinary lives, those produced by **ethnographers**. The ethnography of British youth, the painstaking description of how young people organise and make sense of their daily lives, has a long history (Pearl Jephcott's pioneering study of *Girls Growing Up* was published in 1942; Peter Willmott's classic description of *Adolescent Boys of East London* came out in 1966) but its recurrent finding is that young people are more aware of **constraints** than **freedom**. Ethnographers have therefore been concerned to show how the **rules** of teenage life are constructed and learnt.

Analysing youth cultures in terms of rules of behaviour helps us to clarify the differences between boys and girls – they are subject to different rules. In *Disclosures to a Stranger*, for example, Tom Kitwood shows how class and sex differences affect teenagers' negotiations with their parents about 'going out'. Middle class boys have to persuade their parents that going out won't interfere with their studies or bring them to harm; working class boys have to persuade their parents that they won't get into trouble; girls, of both classes, have, in addition, to convince their parents that they won't be at risk of **sexual activity**. The problematic relationship between leisure and sexuality is thus built into the ways in which girls are expected to regulate their 'free time'. Boys are protected by the sexual double standard – parents are much less concerned about their sons' sex lives. The contrast is indicated by the different implications of saying 'he got into trouble' (with the police) and 'she got into trouble' (she's pregnant).

Different sexual rules thus affect the meaning of 'free time' itself. Empirical evidence suggests, for example, that boys have **more** free time than girls. Girls take on domestic obligations from an early age, have to help their mothers and contribute to household tasks. As Kitwood puts it: 'There is a continuity in home life, between the roles of schoolgirl, daughter-who-goes-out-to-work, wife and wife-who-goes-out-to-work.' And different norms within the family shape leisure possibilities outside it. Boys' free time is mostly enjoyed outside the home; girls, even in their leisure time, come under continuing family authority – have to say where they are going, be back at earlier times, and so on. Given that youth sub-cultures are usually described as street cultures, it is, again, worth noting the conventional implications of saying that a girl or woman is 'on the streets'.

Even in leisure time, then, there are different social constraints acting on boys and girls. They are expected to enjoy themselves in different ways (which are certainly not the results of different biological or psychological needs). Ethnographical studies suggest, in particular, that a highly important aspect of girls' leisure is **having or not having a boy friend**. As girls grow up, they break with 'teenybop culture', shift interest from sports and hobbies to the pursuit of 'femininity', a concern with clothes and make-up and display. Boys don't seem to experience the same sort of break. Their interests remain much the same through puberty; they still go out and about with their mates. If boy friends are central to girls' interests, girl friends are marginal to boys'. Being 'a girlfriend' means being on the fringes of male activities (watching them play football or rehearse with a band, hanging on to the back of a bike, cheering-on a fight), while also being excluded from leisure activities of one's own – 'a girlfriend' is not supposed to go out with anyone else.

Even girls without boyfriends are constrained by the need to have one – which may rule out some activities because they are seen as 'unfeminine' (like getting drunk) or 'childish' (like being involved in hobbies, youth clubs or even school work). As Diana Leonard observed in her study of girls in Wales, *Sex and Generation*, 'They give up going to youth clubs because their interests are not catered for, because they feel they are under instruction ("and they can't teach you kissing there") and because boys who go to youth clubs are either not interested in girls, or not interested in them in the context of the youth club'.

It is important to stress that ethnographic studies don't suggest that teenagers always obey these rules or agree to these expectations. The point is, rather, that they know that they exist and have to take account of them. Of course the rules can be and often are broken, but such rule breaking is a source of anxiety, can mean teenagers feeling isolated, treated as 'weird' by their peers. To grow up 'extraordinary' needs political (as well as sub-cultural) support (a feminist group, for example). Growing up 'ordinary', by contrast, is growing up according to the pervasive **commercial** and **media** ideas of masculinity and femininity. Even Abrams's original market research showed that boys spent their money on immediate pleasures – cigarettes, drink, travel, while girls saved up for more substantial 'feminine' goods – clothes, shoes, cosmetics, hair-dos. A more recent market research study, Susie Fisher and Susan Holder's *Too Much Too Young?* explains this with this quote: 'Boys, everything you do is for boys, you don't want spots for boys, you want to look nice for boys and you take more care over yourself when there's a boy you fancy.'

Boys, it seems, are much less anxious about attracting girls. Even the sub-cultural stylists, who do pay detailed attention to how they look, are primarily concerned to impress their male friends. In the words of a 1960s mod: 'When you were at work you were a nobody. So when you put on your suede or mohair suit and Desert Boots and go to the dance hall, you want to be a somebody to your mates. It's your mates you want to impress, not the girls. You make a statement through your clothes, or your dancing, or your scooter. You had to be cool. To be chasing birds was seen as soft, a bit sentimental. You didn't want to lose face with the other guys.'

One conclusion from this sort of evidence is that peer groups, which are central to sociological accounts of youth, actually play quite different roles for boys and girls. The tension between peer group activities and courtship or sexual pairing is thus resolved differently for the different sexes. Males remain committed to their friendship groups, only have special nights out 'with the girlfriend'; girls 'grow out' of peer group activities and develop instead intense friendships with just one or two other girls. 'Best friends' support each other in the tricky negotiations about leisure and sexual behaviour with both parents and boys.

There is a paradox in the apparent subordination of female leisure to the 'boyfriend problem'. Boyfriends don't seem to be enjoyed much (sexually or otherwise) for their own sake. As Leonard puts it: 'For girls there is little sense of enjoying the time **when one is young and free**, or enjoying a relationship for what it is at a particular time – there is always a concern with where a relationship is leading, and with getting **married**.'

It follows that getting and keeping a suitable boyfriend is a matter of hard work and considerable worry, involves the recurring problem of managing sexuality, deciding 'how far to go'. Boys are (publicly, at any rate) exempted from such anxiety. Not having a girlfriend is less of a social stigma than not having a boyfriend; teenage culture still treats male sexuality as unproblematic: 'boys are after only one thing!' What ethnographic studies show, in short, is that while having a boyfriend is the focus of female leisure activity, it is not a source of much pleasure. What girls say they most enjoy is 'having a good laugh, just doing what you want to do', and that means enjoying oneself **without boys** (disco dancing in female groups, for example). As one of Angela McRobbie's teenagers told her: 'Well, if I had to choose between a boy and me mate, I'd choose her anytime. You know, all they're interested in is if you'll give it to them – and when you don't they pack it in.'

Learning To Be A Teenager

Detailed studies of teenage leisure suggest that many of the activities that are described as 'fun and freedom' are experienced in terms of anxiety and constraint. Most boys do, though 'choose' to behave like boys (even if they're therefore frightened or bored), and most girls do 'choose' the effort of getting and keeping a boyfriend over the pleasure of having laughs with their girl friends. Why?

The issue here is youth culture as a form of **socialisation**, as the setting in which girls and boys learn to be 'feminine' and 'masculine' in preparation for their adult roles. Why, then, are supposedly 'autonomous' or 'deviant' youth groups the setting for such conformist norms of behaviour?

In answering this, most sociologists have examined the ways in which young people are manipulated **ideologically**. Feminist writers like Germaine Greer, Sheila Rowbotham and Sue Sharpe have paid particular attention to the ideology of romance and femininity. The fashion industry, for example (boutiques and chain stores, cosmetics and clothing corporations) invests millions of pounds every year to hard-sell the latest versions of 'glamour' and 'attractiveness'. However female fashions change, their purpose doesn't – to make women desirable to men. Girls' books and magazines like *Jackie* and *Honey* combine this presentation of feminity with the enticement of romantic fictions, which suggest that the purpose of life is the emotional charge provided by 'falling in love'. Youth cultural activities themselves, music making for example, situate the sexes differently: boys become musicians, technicians, experts; girls are fans.

The ideology of femininity suggests that to be a desirable, successful or even recognisable woman means looking, acting and thinking in certain ways. It is such an overwhelming ideology in our society that to preserve some sense of their social significance girls have to collude with the ideology, to make decisions about themselves that go along with the suggestion that to be a teenage girl means to attract teenage boys. The ideology of femininity is, in short, a **patriarchal ideology**. It supports men's power over women and there is little evidence that sub-cultures **resist** such power.

This approach to youth culture implies that ideology is something which is applied 'from the top down' – young people's values derive from the influence of the mass media, parents, adult common sense. But we can approach teenage ideology from the opposite end, as a system of ideas generated by young people themselves in response to their **material** conditions. Thus, even as teenagers, girls and boys are placed differently in social institutions because of the projected division of their adult roles – boys as breadwinners, girls as wives and mothers. Equalities of opportunity legislation may change some of the more obvious school differences (girls doing domestic science, boys doing woodwork and so on) but they remain crucial in the youth labour market. For example, the few girls who get apprenticeships are likely to get them in hairdressing; the few girls who get professional qualifications are likely to get them in nursing. Unskilled girls are more likely to be unemployed than unskilled boys. Unskilled girls who do get jobs get jobs without training, with sparse prospects of career advancement or the acquisition of authority.

In the light of this sort of evidence, it can be argued that, at least for unskilled female school leavers, marriage and motherhood are crucial **occupations**, involve girls' most important **career** choices – marriage will determine both their likely standard of living and their adult status (and, indeed, marriage and motherhood are 'solutions' to girls' experience of unemployment – they offer an instant adult position). The pursuit of boyfriends, potential husbands, is not, therefore, the **result** of romantic ideology, but, rather, romantic ideology is a way of handling the **necessity** of finding 'the right man'. Romance invests the material basis of marriage with a degree of fun and fantasy.

Leisure, Work and Family

I've focussed on studies of female youth in this chapter in order to make a general point. Most sociologists define youth as a **leisure institution**. The analysis of youth cultures and sub-cultures thus focuses on values, on explanations of why young people **choose** to act the ways they do. Descriptions of girls growing up show very vividly, however, that youth cultures are equally a matter of **constraints**. Leisure has to be related to people's situations at work and in the home. Teenagers certainly have possibilities to behave in ways that will be closed off by adult roles and responsibilities, but their leisure is not entirely free, and this has three implications for sub-cultural theory.

First, young people's 'class position' is not just a cultural (or ideological) matter, a question of values. Young people also have specific material positions in the labour market and work place. Even school children are acquiring forms of knowledge and qualification that will determine what sort of jobs they will do, and, in general, there are significant differences in work experience between the employed and the unemployed, the skilled and the unskilled, students and workers. The differences that concern me here are not those between wage rates and leisure resources, but between different sorts of work commitment, satisfaction and expectation, between different sorts of workplace status and discipline. How people experience work (and prepare themselves for it) has significant effects for how they experience leisure (and use it). To make an obvious point, people go out on Friday and Saturday nights because they don't have to go to work on Saturday and Sunday mornings – rhythms of work (student patterns of reading, lectures, seminars and exams vs worker patterns of clocking in, the assembly line, rigid tea and lunch breaks) affect rhythms of leisure. And differences in the 'domestic labour market', the household, equally structure the sexual differences in leisure use.

There is a pressing need for sociologists of youth to follow up Paul Willis's thorough study of unskilled boys (*Learning to Labour*) with equally thorough studies of other social groups (skilled boys, students, young women). How do **they** relate work position, family position and leisure? Are their ideas of fun and pleasure the same as those of Willis's 'lads'?

My own belief is that the deviant/conformist distinction that sub-culturalists took from delinquency theory (it is used by Willis too) may not be the best way of understanding youth politics. 'Naughty' teenagers are not the same thing as 'rebellious' teenagers. Sub-culturalists followed the mass media in focusing on **spectacular** youth, but in doing so they missed the subtler ways in which young people resist and seek to **change** their situation.

This leads to my second point. In common sense terms, political 'resistance' refers to the activities of **organised** groups, with **explicit** demands and arguments and structures. Sub-culturalists made the important point that, in youth culture, resistance can also have a symbolic dimension, involve **implicit** gestures of style. But they seem then to imply that this is the **most** significant form of youth politics. It appears that non-political stylists like mods 'resist' dominant norms, while counter-cultural stylists like hippies do not. But this is to discount not just middle class youth politics, but also those youth struggles (round issues like housing, work, student rights, women, CND, the police, drug laws) which involve **cross-class** alliances. Is **organised** politics middle class (and therefore part of the dominant ideology) by definition? Political youth groups may or may not be important, but we certainly need to be able to analyse their relationship to sub-cultural styles.

Finally, a word on **fantasy**. In reading youth styles for signs and symbols of **collective** consciousness, the sub-cultural approach under-estimates the **individual** joy of dressing up, inventing an image, striking poses. This is a point made in the most entertaining of the sub-cultural studies, Dick Hebdige's *Sub-Culture: The Meaning of Style*. Hebdige suggests that styles are as much gestures of individual imagination as of class expression, relate to people's fantasies as well as to their reality. Thus suburban sixth formers dress up in the imagery of street gangs and play punk and reggae records; working class youth idolise David Bowie, invent their own night clubs, act out scenarios of art and bohemia, dress up as the 'new romantics'.

Sociologists can't, despite the sub-culturalist efforts, judge a style by its cover. Leisure is an alternative to reality as well as a way of expressing it, involves magic for its own sake as well as 'magical solutions to ideological problems'. Young people certainly do seek to inhabit worlds (the pub, the club, the disco floor) in which they are in control. But so do adults, who also indulge in leisure, use it as a source of fantasy, a place to act out 'subterranean values'. The distinctive nature of youth culture must be explained, then, not by reference to leisure itself, but to young people's position in work and family, to the 'reality' from which leisure is, on occasion, an escape.

Chapter Seven
The Future of Youth

The Consequences of Youth Unemployment

In the last chapter, I suggested that one of the limitations of the socio-logy of youth is that it has been, predominantly, a sociology of youth leisure. There have been numerous theoretical disagreements about what youth leisure means, but empirical studies have focused on young people's free time activities. There are good methodological reasons for this: teenagers' public, collective behaviour (and misbehaviour) is easier to observe systematically than their individual dealings with people at home and work. But the focus on leisure has obvious draw-backs. In the last decade, for example, the most important youth issue in Britain (and most other capitalist countries) has been **youth unemployment**. What can leisure sociologists say about this?

Some writers have been tempted simply to equate unemployment and leisure, to conclude that worklessness will intensify young people's commitment to youth culture. This conclusion is, indeed, reflected in successive British governments' policy responses to youth unemploy-ment. The Youth Opportunities and Youth Training Schemes were designed, at least in part, to keep young people occupied, to meet the fear that 'idle' youth are 'mischievous' youth (although there is little statistical evidence for this). It is assumed, in short, that without work school leavers are trapped in their marginal social status. The anxiety is that they will become so embedded in youth cultural pleasures that they'll never be willing to grow up.

There are two immediate problems with this argument. First, leisure has to be defined in **contrast** to work, 'free' time is experienced in contrast to disciplined time (whether in school or occupation) – no work doesn't mean all play. Second, unemployment is not experienced

collectively like leisure. Social psychological research suggests that even though most young unemployed people know that everyone around them is out of work too, they still regard their own situation as an **individual** problem (and certainly not a matter of 'free' choice or 'free' time). Unemployment means staying in bed, hanging around the house, watching day time television or the video, kicking a ball against the wall, boredom; it does not mean spreading into weekday time peer groups' evening and weekend public jaunts.

The sociological implication of this is that the consequence of mass youth unemployment is **not** the intensification of previous youth cultural patterns but **a redefinition of working class youth experience** such that the traditional concept of 'youth' may cease to be relevant to it. In the 1950s and 1960s, when sociological theories of youth were first developed in Britain, the majority of young people left school at 15, went straight to work, earned relatively good money and had a marked degree of independence in both the home and the labour market. In the 1980s the majority of young people leave school at 16, become un-employed or enter short-term training schemes, have a relatively low income and a marked degree of dependence on both their parents and the welfare state. What does this shift in experience mean sociologically?

Youth as an Institution

Sociologists have, conventionally, focused on the 'subjectivity' of youth; they've been interested in how and why young people **construct themselves** as a particular group or culture or style. But youth is also an **effect** of other people's activities, is constructed as a particular role or structural position or institution in society by market forces, state policies and family expectations. Mass youth unemployment, in par-ticular, can't be understood in terms of young people's own choices or even as just a statistical effect of the general economic recession. Young people seem to be specifically unemployable, and in understanding why we can also understand how 'youth' is constructed as a particular category in the labour market.

The question is simple. Why don't employers want 'young workers'? Why, given the choice, do they employ adults? One common answer is that young people these days don't have the right skills and aptitudes. This leads on to a critique of the school system (hence the call in the last few years for a more 'relevant' school curriculum and exam system) but a close inspection of the skills required by industry and instilled in school leavers by Manpower Services Commission (MSC) training schemes suggests that what's at issue is not really formal knowledge or a specific craft. One feature of youth unemployment is, indeed, the decline in the number of apprenticeships, and what employers seem to want is a set of **personal qualities** – responsibility, self-discipline, flexibility, punctuality and so on. These are the 'life skills' which adult workers have acquired through experience. In the labour market, then, a 'young' worker means an **inexperienced** worker.

The contemporary emphasis on experience needs to be understood in its historical context. In the 1960s industrial sociologists carried out a number of empirical studies of 'the transition from school to work'. One of the objects of this research was to improve the careers service, to make job placement more efficient, but even these sociologists were surprised by how long it took school leavers of both sexes to settle down into a particular job or workplace. The transition from school to work meant, in practice, a couple of years of continuous labour movement. Young people left jobs (and were sacked) for essentially trivial reasons; employers took it for granted that to be a young unskilled worker was to have a **casual** attitude to employment (trainees and apprentices were, by contrast, committed to their position). Becoming an adult worker meant, then, a period of **experiment** in the workplace itself.

From this perspective, the rise of youth unemployment means a decline in the demand for 'casual' labour, a decrease in the opportunity for school leavers to experiment with work. The reasons for this must be found in changes in the production process itself. I can only indicate these here but think, for example, of current shifts in the overall shape of the British economy – the decline of steel manufacture and the shipyards, the slump in construction, the expansion of the service sector and micro-electronics business. Even within established companies, technological change, the increasing use of computer-based processes, means a declining demand for **purely** manual skills, for workers with sheer physical strength, courage and stamina. What's happening is a process of 'semi-skilling', a declining demand for traditional crafts (and apprentices) but a rising need for workers who can be trusted with and adapt themselves to expensive electronic machinery. The only employer left, it seems, who still needs unattached, physically fit, 'macho' young labour is the army.

To be a worker now means to be an adult worker, an experienced worker. Employers almost exclusively want settled, responsible employees who can adapt to change on the job and don't require the expense of training (and thus girls find themselves losing in the job competition to the increasing number of married women returning to work). And if school leavers can no longer acquire work discipline simply by getting a job, then state agencies have to step in to provide it – hence the development of Youth Training Schemes.

The most significant consequence of youth unemployment, in short, is the reorganisation of the transition from school to work. If to become a 'young worker' once meant to take an important step towards adult status, now it means increasingly to be a trainee, one's adult status clearly postponed. Two aspects of this should be stressed in particular.

First, the sharpening differentiation between adult and young workers has a significant economic effect. The assumption now is that employers will only take on school leavers (whose inexperience supposedy makes them less productive and more troublesome than adult workers) if they are much cheaper. One purpose of the MSC training policy is to feed young people into the labour market (via state subsidies and the various work experience and job opportunity programmes) as **cheap** labour.

Second, as trainees, young workers have a distinctively low status in the work place itself. They are excluded from trade unions and collective bargaining, they are subject to school-like forms of discipline and control, they are, indeed, dependent on the state for work in the first place. Such 'work experience' is **not** a source of adult status.

To summarise: the direct consequence of wide-scale youth unemployment is to give school leavers a new institutional position, as cheap, dependent labour, clearly demarcated from both adult workers and their peers in further and higher education. This seems a very different position than that occupied by 1950s and 1960s working class teenagers, who had money in their pockets, jobs to choose from, were irresponsible and cocky as they set the leisure pace for everyone else.

Youth as Ideology

What are the implications of changing youth experience for the ideology of youth? In some respects youth unemployment simply widens the existing gap between the commercial image of youth (the poster pictures of freedom, mobility and affluence) and most young people's day-to-day experience of the constraints of work and home and neighbourhood. As David Downes showed in *The Delinquent Solution,* there was always a sector of working class youth for whom 'teenage culture' was inaccessible. Such young people lacked the resources for 'success' in teenage terms as well as for success in school or work terms, hence their 'delinquent solution' to the problems of prestige and self-esteem.

But it can also be argued that the public concern about youth unemployment (reflected in successive governments' youth policies) has had an effect on media images of youth more generally. The established tension between youth as ideal and youth as threat has been overlaid by a new awareness of youth as victim. Press and politicians refer routinely, for example, to 'a wasted generation', to young people being 'thrown on the scrapheap'. It is interesting to observe how young people are addressed as an audience (and as an interest group) by television's increasing number of 'youth programmes', which try to be both entertaining (in their emphasis on pop music and fashion and dance) and serious (in their concern with young people's difficulties in getting jobs or housing or leisure resources). The 1981 'riots', to cite another example, were interpreted not just as an extreme form of delinquent behaviour but also as an understandable, **political** response by young people to their economic and social situation. From being an object of adult envy, youth have become, it seems, an object of adult pity.

The End of Youth Culture?

The concept of 'youth culture' has always had a wider function in society than as simply a term of sociological description. It has acted too as a sort of public fantasy, a model for everyone of leisure consumption, of **how to have a good time**. This idea of youth culture has its origins in the 1920s when the middle class youth world of flappers and jazz and dance was first established as a media image. The youthful interest in fashion and change and up-to-dateness, young people's use of style to establish in-group membership, became themes for all consumption. Advertisers used youthful images of sexiness, sophistication and carelessness to sell goods which in reality had nothing to do with youth culture at all.

Youth culture, in short, is an aspect of a more general consumer culture in which people are encouraged to buy goods with the suggestion that their possession can keep you young. People have no real human or subsistence **need** to buy fashion clothes or furniture, to drink cocktails or Coca-Cola, to smoke or make-up, to choose one particular make of car rather than another. The purchase of such 'luxuries' is thus seen by advertisers as essentially irrational, based on fantasy not reason, and so, for the last fifty years, the 'irrationality' of adult pleasure has been sold in association with the spontaneity and **fun** of being young. This was the flappers' message in the 1920s and it was a message that spread down the social structure to the 'affluent 50s' and 'swinging 60s'.

The question is what happens to such advertising imagery when the meaning of youth as a social category shifts from irresponsibility and **choice** to uselessness and **constraint**, when the young are widely thought of not as an enviable consumer group but as a disturbing labour problem?

It's too soon to answer this question sensibly (and for the moment the commercial image of youth is still obvious in magazines and on advertising hoardings). But some people within the teenage industry itself (the pop and fashion business) are talking about 'the end of teenage' or 'the death of youth' and so one sociological comment should be made. As long as young people are defined and treated as a specific social category, so they will develop (according to their class and gender positions) a 'youth culture', a way of making sense of their situation. What, if anything, will change is that this youth culture will no longer play the part it has in the past for adults too.

Final Questions

Sociologists are no more able than anyone else to ignore common meanings of youth culture, and so it is not surprising, perhaps, that in Britain so much of the academic work on youth has been done by people (like myself) who were teenagers in the late 1950s and early 1960s, who grew up on rock 'n' roll and had their own fantasies of teenage life. But history doesn't stop for sociologists' convenience and it is worth remembering that the 'youth' who feature in the sociology books, the delinquents and affluent teenagers of the 1950s, the sub-culturalists of the 1960s, are now parents, as little able to help their children cope with youth unemployment as their parents were able to help them cope with teenage affluence.

Sociologists can learn from such parental doubts and anxieties. It is always tempting to take a set of categories developed to make sense of one historical moment and to apply them to another historical moment, as if sociological concepts had a permanent, ahistorical power. The implication of this approach to youth is that rising unemployment means rising sub-cultural activity, an increase in delinquency, a dole-queue version of traditional teenage culture. Is there evidence for such conclusions? On the whole (and despite the riots) Britain has absorbed the fact of permanent mass youth unemployment with remarkably little public difficulty (though what goes on within the privacy of the family is another question).

This doesn't mean, though, that there aren't significant changes going on in how young people interpret their situation. It can be argued that one effect of the recession has been to sharpen the class differences among the young. The 1960s notion of the 'classless' youth culture certainly seems irrelevant to the increasing educational gap between those young people who are being made 'relevant' to industry and those who are preparing for higher education, for professional, career qualifications. But it is also true that middle class youth, university and polytechnic graduates, are experiencing unemployment too. The 60s hippie ideal of a classless bohemia, a street culture of squats and music making, hustling and the black economy, political and social action, does still have an inner city presence and may, indeed, be growing. And precisely because working class school leavers don't now achieve adult status directly, through their individual efforts in the labour market, but have to move through the collective experience of training, so their lives are beginning to become more like those of students (one effect of unemployment is that more people than ever before are studying, in one way or another, in technical colleges). Such 'student' experience makes possible new sorts of youth organisation, new definitions and demands from youth as an interest not a consumer group. Is it in the 1980s that youth will become, finally, a **political** category?

Bibliography

Abrams, M. *The Teenage Consumer* (Routledge & Kegan Paul, London, 1959)

Allen, S. 'Some theoretical problems in the study of youth', *Sociological Review* 16, 1968

Becker, H. *Outsiders – Studies in the Sociology of Deviance* (Free Press, New York, 1963)

Berger, B. 'On the Youthfulness of Youth Culture', *Social Research*, 30, 1963

Brake, M. *The Sociology of Youth Culture and Youth Subcultures* (Routledge & Kegan Paul, London, 1980)

Burt, C. *The Young Delinquent* (University of London Press, London, 1925)

Casburn, M. *Girls Will Be Girls* (Women's Research and Resources Centre, London, 1979)

Cloward, R. and Ohlin, L.E. *Delinquency and Opportunity* (Free Press, New York, 1960)

Cohen, A.K. *Delinquent Boys – The Subculture of the Gang* (Collier-Macmillan, London, 1955)

Cohen, P. 'Subcultural Conflict and Working Class Community', *Working Papers in Cultural Studies* 2, 1972

Cohen, S. *Folk Devils and Moral Panics* (Paladin, London, 1973)

Coleman, J.S. *The Adolescent Society* (Free Press, New York, 1961)

Cowie, C. and Lees, S. 'Slags or Drags', *Feminist Review* 9, 1981

Cowie, J., Cowie, V. and Slater, E. *Delinquency in Girls* (Heinemann, London, 1968)

Downes, D. *The Delinquent Solution* (Routledge & Kegan Paul, London, 1966)

Eisenstadt, S.N. *From Generation To Generation* (Free Press, Chicago, 1956)

Fass, P.S. *The Damned and the Beautiful. American Youth in the 1920s* (Oxford University Press, New York, 1977)

Fisher, S. and Holder, S. *Too Much Too Young?* (Pan, London, 1981)

Frith, S. *Sound Effects. Youth, Leisure and the Politics of Rock'n'roll* (Constable, London, 1983)

Gillis, J.R. *Youth and History* (Academic Press, New York, 1974)

Greer, G. *The Female Eunuch* (Paladin, London, 1970)

Hall, S. and Jefferson, T. *Resistance Through Rituals* (Hutchinson, London, 1976)

Hall, S. et al *Policing the Crisis* (Macmillan, London, 1978)

Hebdige, D. *Subculture: The Meaning of Style* (Methuen, London, 1979)

Jephcott, P. *Girls Growing Up* (Faber, London, 1942)

Kitwood, T. *Disclosures to a Stranger* (Routledge & Kegan Paul, London, 1980)

Leonard, D. *Sex and Generation* (Tavistock, London, 1980)

McRobbie, A. 'Settling Accounts With Subculture', *Screen Education* 34, 1980

McRobbie, A. 'Working Class Girls and the Culture of Femininity', *Women Take Issue* (Hutchinson, London, 1978)

McRobbie, A. and McCabe, T. *Feminism for Girls* (Routledge & Kegan Paul, London, 1981)

Mannheim, K. *Essays in the Sociology of Knowledge* (Routledge & Kegan Paul, London, 1952)

Marsland, D. *Sociological Explorations in the Service of Youth* (NYB, Leicester, 1978)

Matza, D. and Sykes, G.M. 'Juvenile Delinquency and Subterranean Values' *American Sociological Review* 26, 1961

Matza, D. *Delinquency and Drift* (John Wiley, New York, 1964)

Matza, D. *Becoming Deviant* (Prentice-Hall, New Jersey, 1969)

Mays, J.B. *The Young Pretenders* (Michael Joseph, London, 1965)

Merton, R.K. 'Social Structure and Anomie' *American Sociological Review* 3, 1938

Miller, W.B. 'Lower Class Culture as a Generating Milieu of Gang Delinquency' *Journal of Social Issues* 14, 1958

Nagel, J. *Student Power* (Merlin, London, 1969)

Parker, H. *View From The Boys* (David and Charles, Newton Abbott, 1974)

Parsons, T. 'Age and Sex in the Social Structure of the United States', *American Sociological Review* 7, 1942

Pearson, G. *Hooligan: A History of Respectable Fears* (Macmillan, London, 1983)

Rees, T.L. and Atkinson, P. *Youth Unemployment and State Intervention* (Routledge & Kegan Paul, London, 1982)

Robins, D. and Cohen, P. *Knuckle Sandwich* (Penguin, London, 1978)

Rowbotham, S. *Woman's Consciousness, Man's World* (Penguin, London, 1973)

Sharpe, S. *Just Like A Girl* (Penguin, London, 1976)

Smart, C. and Smart, B. *Women, Sexuality and Social Control* (Routledge & Kegan Paul, London, 1978)

West, D.J. *The Young Offenders* (Penguin, London, 1967)

Whyte, W.F. *Street Corner Society* (University of Chicago Press, Chicago, 1943)

Willis, P. *Learning to Labour* (Saxon House, London, 1977)

Willmott, P. *Adolescent Boys of East London* (Routledge & Kegan Paul, London, 1966)

Index